W9-AJZ-763

teach® yourself

instant french
elisabeth smith

For UK order enquiries: please contact Bookpoint Ltd, 130 Milton Park, Abingdon, Oxon OX14 4SB. Telephone: +44 (0) 1235 827720. Fax: +44 (0) 1235 400454. Lines are open 09.00–18.00, Monday to Saturday, with a 24-hour message answering service. Details about our titles and how to order are available at www.teachyourself.co.uk

For USA order enquiries: please contact McGraw-Hill Customer Services, PO Box 545, Blacklick, OH 43004-0545, USA. Telephone: 1-800-722-4726. Fax: 1-614-755-5645.

For Canada order enquiries: please contact McGraw-Hill Ryerson Ltd, 300 Water St, Whitby, Ontario L1N 9B6, Canada. Telephone: 905 430 5000. Fax: 905 430 5020.

Long renowned as the authoritative source for self-guided learning – with more than 40 million copies sold worldwide – the **teach yourself** series includes over 300 titles in the fields of languages, crafts, hobbies, business, computing and education.

British Library Cataloguing in Publication Data: a catalogue record for this title is available from the British Library.

Library of Congress Catalog Card Number: on file.

First published in UK 1998 by Hodder Education, 338 Euston Road, London, NW1 3BH.

First published in US 1998 by Contemporary Books, a Division of the McGraw-Hill Companies, 1 Prudential Plaza, 130 East Randolph Street, Chicago, IL 60601 USA.

This edition published 2003.

The **teach yourself** name is a registered trade mark of Hodder Headline.

Typeset by Transet Limited, Coventry, England.
Printed in Great Britain for Hodder Education, a division of Hodder Headline, 338 Euston Road, London NW1 3BH, by Cox & Wyman Ltd, Reading, Berkshire.

Hodder Headline's policy is to use papers that are natural, renewable and recyclable products and made from wood grown in sustainable forests. The logging and manufacturing processes are expected to conform to the environmental regulations of the country of origin.

Impression number   10 9 8
Year   2009 2008 2007 2006 2005

contents

If, like me, you usually skip introductions, don't turn the page. Read on! You need to know how **Instant French** works and why.

When I decided to write the **Instant** series I first called it *Barebones*, because that's what you want: *no frills, no fuss, just the bare bones and go!* So in **Instant French** you'll find:

- Only 378 words to say everything, well ... nearly everything.

- No ghastly grammar – just a few useful tips.

- No time wasters such as 'the pen of my aunt...'.

- No phrase book phrases for bungee jumping from the Eiffel Tower.

- No need to be perfect. Mistakes won't spoil your success.

I've put some 30 years of teaching experience into this course. I know how people learn. I also know how long they are motivated by a new project (a few weeks) and how little time they can spare to study each day (½ hour). That's why you'll complete **Instant French** in six weeks and get away with 35 minutes a day.

Of course there is some learning to do, but I have tried to make it as much fun as possible, even when it is boring. You'll meet Tom and Kate Walker on holiday in France. They do the kind of things you need to know about: shopping, eating out and getting about. As you will note Tom and Kate speak **Instant French** all the time, even to each other. What paragons of virtue!

To get the most out of this course, there are only two things you really should do:

- Follow the **Day-by-day guide** as suggested. Please don't skip bits and short-change your success. Everything is there for a reason.
- If you are a complete beginner, buy the recording that accompanies this book. It will help you to speak faster and with confidence.

When you have filled in your **Certificate** at the end of the book and can speak **Instant French**, I would like to hear from you. You can write to me care of Hodder & Stoughton Educational.

Elizabeth Smith

how this book works

Instant French has been structured for your rapid success. This is how it works:

Day-by-day guide Stick to it. If you miss a day, add one.

Dialogues Follow Tom and Kate through France. The English of Weeks 1–3 is in 'French-speak' to get you tuned in.

New words Don't fight them, don't skip them – learn them! The flash cards will help you.

Good news grammar After you read it you can forget half and still succeed! That's why it's good news.

Flash words and flash sentences Read about these building blocks in the flash card section on page 80. Then use them!

Learn by heart Obligatory! Memorizing puts you on the fast track to speaking in full sentences.

Let's speak French *You* will be doing the talking – in French.

Spot the keys Listen to rapid French and make sense of it.

Say it simply Learn how to use plain, **Instant French** to say what you want to say. Don't be shy!

Test your progress Mark your own test and be amazed by the result.

Answers This is where you'll find the answers to the exercises.

▶ This icon asks you to switch on the recording.

Pronunciation If you don't know it and don't have the recording go straight to page 17. You need to know about pronunciation before you can start Week 1.

Progress chart Enter your score each week and monitor your progress. Are you going for *very good* or *outstanding*?

Certificate It's on the last page. In six weeks it will have your name on it!

Since **Instant French** was first published the euro has become France's official currency. Occasionally – as in this book and the recording that goes with it – you will still hear people using *francs*.

progress chart

At the end of each week record your test score on the progress chart below.

At the end of the course throw out your worst result – anybody can have a bad week – and add up your *five* best weekly scores. Divide the total by five to get your average score and overall course result.

Write your result – *outstanding, excellent, very good* or *good* – on your **Certificate** at the end of the book.

If you scored more than 80% enlarge it and frame it!

Progress chart

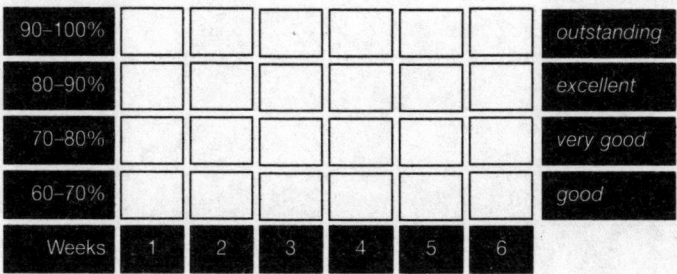

90–100%							outstanding
80–90%							excellent
70–80%							very good
60–70%							good
Weeks	1	2	3	4	5	6	

Total of five best weeks =

divided by five =

Your final result _____ %

01 week one

Study for 35 minutes – or a little longer if you can!

Day zero

- Open the book and read **Read this first**.
- Now read **How this book works**.

Day one

- Read **In the aeroplane**.
- Listen to/Read **Dans l'avion**.
- Listen to/Read the **New words**, then learn some of them.

Day two

- Repeat **Dans l'avion** and **New words**.
- Listen to/Read **Pronunciation**.
- Learn more **New words**.
- Use the **Flash words** to help you.

Day three

- Learn all the **New words** until you know them well.
- Read and learn the **Good news grammar**.

Day four

- Cut out and learn the ten **Flash sentences**.
- Listen to/Read **Let's speak French**.

Day five

- Listen to/Read **Let's speak French** once again.
- Listen to/Read **Learn by heart**.

Day six

- Translate **Test your progress**.

Day seven is your day off!

day-by-day guide

In the aeroplane

Tom and Kate Walker are on their way to France. They are boarding flight QS 16 to Marseille via Paris and squeeze past Henri Cardin.

Tom   Excuse me, we have the seats 9a and 9b.

Henri   Ah, yes, one moment please.

Tom   Hello. We are Tom and Kate Walker.

Henri   Good day. My name is Cardin.

Tom   Pierre Cardin?

Henri   No, unfortunately. I am Henri Cardin.

Tom   We are going to Marseille. You too?

Henri   No, I am going to Paris but I am from Toulouse.

Tom   I was in Toulouse in May. Toulouse is very beautiful. I was in Toulouse for the work.

Henri   What do you do?

Tom   I work with computers.

Henri   And you, Mrs Walker? What do you do?

Kate   I was at Mobil. Now I work at Rover. It is better.

Henri   Are you from London?

Kate   No, we are from Manchester. We were one year in New York and three years in London. We are now in Birmingham.

Henri   I was at Renault. Now I work for the Bank of France.

Tom   Have you a good job at the bank?

Henri   The work is not interesting but well paid. I need a lot of money. I have a big house, a Mercedes and four children. My wife is American. She has her parents in Los Angeles and a girlfriend in Dallas, and she is always on the telephone. It is very expensive.

Kate   We are on holiday. You too?

Henri   No, unfortunately. My holidays are in September. We are going to Provence but without the children. We have a house in St Tropez – without telephone!

▶ Dans l'avion

Tom and Kate Walker are on their way to France. They are boarding flight QS 16 to Marseille via Paris and squeeze past Henri Cardin.

Tom	Excusez-moi, nous avons les places neuf a et neuf b.
Henri	Ah oui, un moment s'il vous plaît.
Tom	Bonjour. Nous sommes Tom et Kate Walker.
Henri	Bonjour. Mon nom est Cardin.
Tom	Pierre Cardin?
Henri	Non, malheureusement. Je suis Henri Cardin.
Tom	Nous allons à Marseille. Vous aussi?
Henri	Non, je vais à Paris mais je suis de Toulouse.
Tom	J'étais à Toulouse en mai. Toulouse est très beau. J'étais à Toulouse pour le travail.
Henri	Que faites-vous?
Tom	Je travaille avec des ordinateurs.
Henri	Et vous, Madame Walker? Que faites-vous?
Kate	J'étais chez Mobil. Actuellement, je travaille chez Rover. C'est mieux.
Henri	Vous êtes de Londres?
Kate	Non, nous sommes de Manchester. Nous étions un an à New York et trois ans à Londres. Nous sommes actuellement à Birmingham.
Henri	J'étais chez Renault. Actuellement je travaille pour la Banque de France.
Tom	Avez-vous un bon poste à la banque?
Henri	Le travail n'est pas intéressant mais bien payé. J'ai besoin de beaucoup d'argent. J'ai une grande maison, une Mercédès et quatre enfants. Ma femme est américaine. Elle a ses parents à Los Angeles et une amie à Dallas, et elle est toujours au téléphone. C'est très cher.
Kate	Nous sommes en vacances. Vous aussi?
Henri	Non, malheureusement. Mes vacances sont en septembre. Nous allons en Provence mais sans les enfants. Nous avons une maison à St Tropez – sans téléphone!

▶ New words

Learn your vocabulary by covering up the French words. Then go down the list of the English words and see how many you can remember. Always say the French words OUT LOUD.

dans *in, inside*
le, la, l', les *the*
l'avion *the aeroplane*
excusez-moi *excuse me*
nous *we*
nous avons *we have*
les places *the seats*
neuf *nine*
a, b pronounce *'ah', 'bay'*
et *and*
oui *yes*
un moment *a/one moment*
s'il vous plaît *please*
bonjour *good day, good morning, good afternoon, hello*
nous sommes *we are*
mon, ma, mes *my*
le nom *the name*
est *is*
non *no*
malheureusement *unfortunately*
je *I*
je suis *I am*
nous allons *we go, we are going*
à *to, at*
vous *you* (polite)
aussi *also, too*
je vais *I go, I am going*
mais *but*
de *of, from*
j'étais *I was*
en *in, at*
mai *May*
très *very*
beau, belle *beautiful*
pour *for*

le travail *the work*
que *what*
que faites-vous? *what do you do?*
je travaille *I work*
avec *with*
(des) ordinateurs *computers*
Madame *Mrs*
chez *at*
actuellement *now, at present*
c'est *it is, this is*
mieux *better*
vous êtes *you are* (polite)
nous étions *we were*
un, une *a*
un an, les ans *a year, the years*
trois *three*
avez-vous? *do you have?* (polite)
bon, bonne *good*
un poste *a post, position, job*
la banque *the bank*
ne...pas *not*
intéressant(e) *interesting*
bien payé *well paid*
j'ai *I have*
j'ai besoin de *I have need of, I need*
beaucoup *much, a lot of*
l'argent, d'argent *the money, of money*
grand(e) *big*
une maison *a house*
quatre *four*
les enfants *the children*
la femme *the wife, woman*
américain(e) *American*
elle *she, it*

a *has*	cher, chère *expensive*
ses parents *his/her parents*	les vacances *the holidays*
une amie *a girlfriend*	sont *are*
toujours *always*	septembre *September*
au téléphone *on the telephone*	sans *without*

TOTAL NEW WORDS: 78
...only 300 words to go!

Some extra words

les mois (the months)
janvier, février, mars, avril, mai, juin, juillet, août, septembre,
octobre, novembre, décembre

les numéros (numbers)
zéro,	un,	deux,	trois,	quatre,	cinq,	six,	sept,	huit,	neuf,	dix
0	1	2	3	4	5	6	7	8	9	10

More greetings
Salut! *Hi!*, **Allô! Hello!**, *Ça va? How are you?*, **Bonsoir** *Good evening*,
Bonne nuit *Good night*, **Au revoir** *Goodbye*.

Good news grammar

This is the good news part of each week. Remember, I promised:
no ghastly grammar! I simply explain the differences between
English and French. This will help you to speak French **Instantly**!

1 Names of things – nouns

There are two kinds of nouns in French: *masculine* and
feminine.

You can tell which is which by the word **le** or **la** (*the*), or **un** or
une (*a* or *one*) in front of the word.

Le poste or **un** poste is masculine. La maison or **une** maison is
feminine.

If you add an adjective to describe the job or the house, the
adjective also becomes masculine or feminine. This means that
there are two versions of every adjective!

Example le poste est **bon**   une **bonne** maison

Other examples are: **cher** and **chère**, **grand** and **grande**, **intéressant** and **intéressante**. But it's **beau** and **belle**. (Sorry!)

As you can see, it's not that bad! You usually just add an **e** if the nouns starts with **la** or **une**.

When talking about more than one thing, you use **les** and add an **s** to the noun and adjectives: Les postes sont bons. Les maisons sont bonnes.

Confused? Here is the Good News: in **Instant French** mistakes are allowed. If you say 'le maison est grand', nobody will worry!

2 Doing things – verbs

This is a bit of 'bad news' in French, so brace yourself. When you want to say in French: *I work, you work, we work, he works*, or *they work*, the ending of the word **travailler** (*to work*) changes almost every time. And worse: some verbs change altogether. If you want to say: *I have, you have*, or *we have* – it's a completely different word every time!

But don't despair! Start off with learning **travailler** which is a regular paid up member of the good verbs team (-**er** verbs). These verbs all share the same endings, so know one, know lots!

Next learn **avoir** (*to have*). You'll use it every day.

travailler – *work*		**avoir** – *have*	
je travaille	*I work*	j'ai	*I have*
vous travaillez	*you work*	vous avez	*you have*
nous travaillons	*we work*	nous avons	*we have*
il travaille	*he, it works*	il a	*he, it has*
elle travaille	*she, it works*	elle a	*she, it has*
ils, elles travaillent	*they work*	ils, elles ont	*they have*

In spoken French **travaille** and **travaillent** sound the same, so just remember **travaillons** and **travaillez**: easy!

Il and **elle** can both mean *it*: Le poste – il est bon. La maison – elle est bonne. 'It is good', in each case.

3 How to say: not

When you want to say *not* in French, e.g. I am *not* in Paris, you use two words: **ne** and **pas**.

You wrap them around your verb, **ne** in front and **pas** behind it: Je **ne** suis **pas** à Paris. Le travail **n**'est **pas** intéressant.

▶ Pronunciation

French pronunciation is very different from English pronunciation and quite complicated, so **please buy the recording**. It makes learning far easier and you'll be speaking French much faster.

But perhaps you just need a refresher – so here come the rules!

1 Single vowels

The English word in brackets gives you an example of the sound. Say the sound OUT LOUD, and then the French examples OUT LOUD.

Remember with **Instant French**: near enough is good enough.

a	(*us*)	à, place, quatre, vacances
e	(*yes*)	le, je, est, elle
é, è, ê	(*say*)	étais, très, êtes
i, y	(*fee*)	Nice, dix, avril, y
o	(*not*)	non, bon, poste
u		There is no English equivalent. Try the way a Scotsman would say 'noo' in 'och aye the *noo*'. Then say **une, excusez**.

2 Doubles and triples

These make only one sound.

ai, aî, ei	(*say*)	maison, j'ai, mais, faites, étais, plaît, neige (*snow*)
au, eau, ô	(*no*)	au, aussi, beau, Renault, Côte
eu	(*curve*)	deux, ordinateur, malheureusement
ou, aoû	(*June*)	nous, pour, bonjour, épouse, Toulouse, août

3 Now some vowel combinations

These are pronounced one at a time.

oi	(*No-ah*)	moi, trois, revoir
oui	(*Lou-is*)	oui
ui	('oo-ee')	suis (If you say this quickly, it sounds like 'swee')
ieu	('ee-ur')	mieux

4 Vowel and consonant combinations: *er* and *ez*

You will meet them at the end of words. They are pronounced as one sound, like 'ay' in *play*. The r and z are not pronounced. Now say: **aller, chez, excusez**.

5 Here come some 'unusuals'

These are unusual because they are said as if you have a cold, and your nose is blocked. They are mostly found at the end of words.

an, en am, em	(*sung*)	dans, en, moment, septembre
in, im	(*sang*)	Cardin, cinq
on, om	(*song*)	bon, bonjour, nom, allons, maison
un, um	('-urng')	un

6 A few consonants

Only these consonants are different in French.

ç	this strange letter sounds like a double 's': **garçon**
h	this is silent: **mal(h)eureusement, (h)omme**
j, g	before e and i like *j* in *jolly*, but softer: **j'ai, jour, Peugeot**
ll	like *y* in *yes*: **travaille**
qu	like *k* in *king*: **que, banque, quatre**
s	sometimes soft like an English *z*: **maison**
ch	like *sh* in *ship*: **chez**
r	a dry, 'throaty' version of the English *r*: **trois**

7 Finally, silent endings

This is where French is very different from other European languages. Quite a lot of it is not pronounced. Whenever you come across the following letters, usually at the end of a word – just swallow them. They must not be heard!

s	Silent at the end of many French words. Look at these: **dans, avons, vous, suis, Paris, mais, trois** and **toujours**.
t, ts	Both are silent at the end of a word: **et, sont, enfants**. Note: in **est** both s and t are silent; just pronounce the e.
z, x	Both are silent at the end of a word: **chez, beaux, mieux**.
es	Both are silent: **places, sommes, faites, vacances**. But in **les, des, très** only the s is silent. Say: 'lay', 'day', 'tray'.
e	Many words end in silent e: **appelle, belle, femme**. But e is heard when it has an accent: **terminé** and in words of one syllable: **de, je, le**.

8 Why French sounds 'smooth'

This is because those silent letters at the end of words are pulled across to the next word. So **nous avons** will sound like 'nousavons'. Here are three more examples: **vous aussi, trois ans, nous allons**.

Many words are contracted. When two vowels collide one is dropped: **je étais** becomes **j'étais** and **ce est** becomes **c'est**. ...**C'est si bon!**

You have just studied 50 sounds and 10 exceptions, and you are entitled to be totally confused! Why not buy the recording.

▶ Let's speak French

I shall give you ten English sentences and you'll put them into French. Always speak OUT LOUD. After each one check the answer at the bottom of the page. Tick it if you got it right. If you have the recording, listen to check your answers to **Let's speak French**.

1 My name is Walker.
2 You are from London?
3 Yes, I am from London.
4 I have a girlfriend in Nice.
5 We are going to Toulouse.

6 Do you have a Mercedes?
7 No, unfortunately (not).
8 We have a house in Calais.
9 The work is well paid.
10 You are on holiday?

Well, how many did you get right? If you are not happy, do it again! Here are some questions in French. Answer each one in French – OUT LOUD, checking as you go. Start every answer with **oui** and **nous**.

11 Vous êtes de Manchester?
12 Vous avez une maison à Londres?
13 Vous avez besoin d'un poste?
14 Vous travaillez en France?
15 Vous avez quatre enfants?

Now start all your answers with **je** and tell me in French that...

16 you were in Paris in May.
17 you work at Rover.
18 you need a bank.
19 you don't have a computer.
20 you don't have a lot of money.

Answers

1 Mon nom est Walker.
2 Vous êtes de Londres?
3 Oui, je suis de Londres.
4 J'ai une amie à Nice.
5 Nous allons à Toulouse.
6 Avez-vous une Mercédès?
   or: Vous avez une Mercédès?
7 Non, malheureusement.
8 Nous avons une maison à Calais.
9 Le travail est bien payé.
10 Vous êtes en vacances?

11 Oui, nous sommes de Manchester.
12 Oui, nous avons une maison à Londres.
13 Oui, nous avons besoin d'un poste.
14 Oui, nous travaillons en France.
15 Oui, nous avons quatre enfants.
16 J'étais à Paris en mai.
17 Je travaille chez Rover.
18 J'ai besoin d'une banque.
19 Je n'ai pas un ordinateur.
20 Je n'ai pas beaucoup d'argent.

Well, what was your score? For 20/20 take a triple gold star!

▶ Learn by heart

Don't skip this exercise because it reminds you of school... If you want to **speak**, not stumble, learning by heart does the trick! Fill in the gaps with your personal, or any, information.

Mon nom est...

Mon nom est .... (*name*). Je suis de .... (*place*).
J'étais à .... (*place*) en .... (*month*).
Je travaille chez .... (*name of firm*).
Nous avons une belle maison à .... (*place*).
C'est très cher.
En juillet nous allons à .... (*place*).
Êtes-vous aussi en vacances? Non, malheureusement.

Say **Mon nom est...** out loud and fairly fast. Can you beat 40 seconds?

Test your progress

Translate these sentences into French. This is your only written exercise for the week. You'll be amazed how easy it is! Are you going for 90%?

1 Hello, we are Helen and Paul.
2 I am from Marseille. You, too?
3 I was in Cannes in July.
4 My parents have a Rover.
5 We are going to Nice with the Renault and five children.
6 I don't have a good job.
7 I need a house for the holidays.
8 What do you do? Computers?
9 She has two jobs and three telephones.
10 Excuse me, are you Mrs Cardin?
11 We work at Renault. The work is well paid.
12 We have a very expensive computer.
13 I am in France, but without my wife.
14 We were seven months in Paris. That's a lot!
15 I go to Nice. It is very beautiful in April.

The scoring instructions and answers are on page 74. When you have worked out your result, enter it on the Progress chart on page 9.

02

week two

35 minutes – but a little extra will speed up your progress!

23

Day one

- Read **In Provence**.
- Listen to/Read **En Provence**.
- Listen to/Read the **New words**. Learn 20 easy ones.

Day two

- Repeat **En Provence** and the **New words**.
- Repeat **Pronunciation**, if you need to.
- Learn the harder **New words**.
- Use the **Flash words** to help you.

Day three

- Learn all the **New words** until you know them well.
- Read and learn the **Good news grammar**.

Day four

- Cut out and learn the ten **Flash sentences**.
- Listen to/Read **Learn by heart**.

Day five

- Listen to/Read **Let's speak French**.
- Go over **Learn by heart**.

Day six

- Translate **Test your progress**.

Day seven is a study-free day!

day-by-day guide

In Provence

In Marseille Tom and Kate hire a car and drive into the hills of Provence. They speak to Gigi Dupont of Hôtel de la Provence, and later to Emile, the waiter.

Kate   Good afternoon. Have you a room for two for one night and not very expensive, please?

Gigi   Yes we have a little room with bath. But the shower is broken. My husband can perhaps it repair.

Tom   Where is the room?

Gigi   It is here on the left. Is it that it is enough big?

Kate   The room is a little small but not bad. It is how much?

Gigi   Only 300 francs for two but no credit card, please. There is a breakfast from 8 hours to 9 hours and half.

Kate   All right, we take the room, but can we take the breakfast at 8 o'clock less the quarter? We would like to go tomorrow at 8 o'clock and quarter to Nice.

Tom   Another question, where can we take a coffee? Is there a café or a bistro around here?

Gigi   There is a café at five minutes. It is not difficult – 30 metres to the right and then straight ahead.

(In the café)

Emile   What would you like?

Kate   A white coffee and a tea with milk please.

Emile   Would you like to eat something? We have cakes.

Tom   Two, please. One with and one without cream.

Tom   My tea is cold.

Kate   But the coffee is superb.

Tom   The table is too small.

Kate   But the toilets are very clean.

Tom   My cake is not good.

Kate   But the waiter is gorgeous.

Tom   The bill please.

Emile   60 francs, please.

▶ En Provence

In Marseille Tom and Kate hire a car and drive into the hills of Provence. They speak to Gigi Dupont of Hôtel de la Provence, and later to Emile, the 'garçon'.

Kate Bonjour. Avez-vous une chambre pour deux pour une nuit et pas très chère, s'il vous plaît?

Gigi Oui, nous avons une petite chambre avec bain. Mais la douche est en panne. Mon mari peut peut-être la réparer.

Tom Où est la chambre?

Gigi Elle est ici, à gauche. Est-ce qu'elle est assez grande?

Kate La chambre est un peu petite mais pas mal. C'est combien?

Gigi Seulement trois cents francs pour deux, mais pas de carte de crédit, s'il vous plaît. Il y a un petit déjeuner de huit heures à neuf heures et demie.

Kate D'accord, nous prenons la chambre. Mais pouvons-nous prendre le petit déjeuner à huit heures moins le quart? Nous voudrions aller demain à huit heures et quart à Nice.

Tom Une autre question, où pouvons-nous prendre un café? Il y a un café ou un bistrot par ici?

Gigi Il y a un café à cinq minutes. Ce n'est pas difficile – trente mètres à droite et ensuite tout droit.

(Dans le café)

Emile Que désirez-vous?

Kate Un café crème et un thé au lait, s'il vous plaît.

Emile Vous désirez manger quelque chose? Nous avons des gâteaux.

Tom Deux, s'il vous plaît. Un avec et un sans crème fraîche.

Tom Mon thé est froid.

Kate Mais le café est superbe.

Tom La table est trop petite.

Kate Mais les toilettes sont très propres.

Tom Mon gâteau n'est pas bon.

Kate Mais le garçon est adorable.

Tom L'addition, s'il vous plaît.

Emile Soixante francs, s'il vous plaît.

▶ New words

Learning words the traditional way can be boring. If you enjoyed the **Flash cards** why not make your own for the rest of the words. Always say the words OUT LOUD. It's the fast track to speaking!

la chambre *the room*
la nuit *the night*
pas, pas de *no, not*
petit(e) *small*
le bain *the bath*
la douche *the shower*
en panne *broken*
peut-être *perhaps,* lit. *can be*
le mari *the husband*
il peut *he can*
la (on its own) *her, it*
réparer *(to) repair*
où? *where?*
ici, par ici *here, around here*
à gauche *on the left*
est-ce que...? *is it that...?*
(used to start a question)
assez *enough*
un peu *a little*
pas mal *not bad*
combien? *how much, how many?*
seulement *only*
trois cents *300*
le franc *the French franc*
la carte de crédit *the credit card*
il y a *there is, there are*
le petit déjeuner *the breakfast*
de...à *from...to*
huit *eight*
neuf heures *nine hours, nine o'clock*
et demie *and half, half past*
d'accord *all right, agreed*
nous prenons *we take*
nous pouvons *we can*
prendre *(to) take*

moins le quart *less the quarter, quarter to*
nous voudrions *we would like*
aller *(to) go*
demain *tomorrow*
et quart *and quarter, quarter past*
autre *other*
la question *the question*
le café *the coffee, the café*
la minute *the minute*
difficile *difficult*
trente *30*
à droite *on the right*
ensuite *then, next*
tout droit *straight ahead*
le garçon *the waiter, the boy*
vous désirez *you would like*
le café crème *the white coffee*
le thé *the tea*
au lait *with milk*
manger *(to) eat*
quelque chose *something*
le gâteau, des gâteaux *the cake, cakes*
ou *or*
la crème (fraîche) *the cream*
froid(e) *cold*
superbe *super, superb*
la table *the table*
trop *too*
les toilettes *the toilets*
propre *clean*
adorable *adorable, gorgeous*
l'addition *the bill*
soixante *60*

Some useful extras

les numéros (numbers)

11	onze
12	douze
13	treize
14	quatorze
15	quinze
16	seize
17	dix-sept (ten-seven)
18	dix-huit (ten-eight)
19	dix-neuf (ten-nine)
20	vingt
21	vingt et un
22	vingt-deux
30	trente
40	quarante
50	cinquante
60	soixante
70	soixante-dix (60 + 10!)
71	soixante et onze (60 + 11!)
80	quatre-vingts (4 x 20!)
90	quatre-vingt-dix (4 x 20 + 10!)
100	cent

l'heure (time, hour)

à quelle heure?	at what time?
à ... heure/s	at ... o'clock
une minute	a minute
une heure	an hour
un jour	a day
une semaine	a week
un mois	a month
un an	a year
ce matin	this morning
ce soir	this evening

21, 31, 41, 51, 61, 71 all get an extra **et**: twenty and one. The numbers in between are just as in English: 47 quarante-sept.

Here are two important boxes. But don't worry about them today. They are for tomorrow when you've read the **Good news grammar**.

être – *to be*	
je suis	*I am*
vous êtes	*you are*
nous sommes	*we are*
il est	*he is, it is*
elle est	*she is, it is*
ils/elles sont	*they are*

aller – *to go*	
je vais	*I go*
vous allez	*you go*
nous allons	*we go*
il va	*he goes, it goes*
elle va	*she goes, it goes*
ils/elles vont	*they go*

Good news grammar

1 Asking a question – easy!

To ask a question in French you can use your voice to change **Vous avez un bon poste!** into **Vous avez un bon poste?** Or you can turn the words around: **Avez-vous** un bon poste? Put a hyphen in between if you are writing.

You can also start a question using **Est-ce que.** It literally means: *Is it that...?* So you haven't got anywhere except gaining a bit of time for your question. **Est-ce que** (..um..) **vous avez un bain?** If you don't want a mouth full of teeth say: **Vous avez un bain?** It's much easier!

2 *Il y a:* there is, there are – very useful!

You will use this a lot:

Il y a un garçon adorable. **Il y a** des tartes aux fraises.

If you want to ask *is there?* or *are there?* you can either stay with **il y a?**, using your voice to make it sound like a question or turn it around and say **y a-t-il?**

Il y a un café par ici? **Y a-t-il** un café par ici?

If you go for the second option you have to slot in a **t** to make it sound better.

3 *du, de la, d', des*

These are used when you don't want to say *the cakes* or *the coffee*, but simply: *cakes* or *coffee*. So you would say: **des gâteaux** or **du café.**

Good news: If you order 'café avec crème' you'll still get it!

4 *C'est*

This pops up frequently. Remember: **c'est** means both *it is* and *this/that is*:

C'est combien?   C'est bon!

5 *être* and *aller* – you'll use these every day!

Think how often you say *I am...* or *we are going...* I have put the verbs **être** and **aller** into boxes for you. They are on the previous page. Spend 5 minutes on each NOW.

▶ Let's speak French

If you have the recording, use it to check your answers. Here are ten sentences for you to say in French – OUT LOUD!

1 Do you have a double room?
2 Do you have the bill, please?
3 At what time is breakfast?
4 The telephone is broken.
5 Can he repair it?
6 We would like to eat something.
7 Where is the café, on the left or on the right?
8 How much is it?
9 We take it.
10 I work from 9 o'clock to 6 o'clock.

Now answer these questions. Use **oui** where you can:

11 La chambre est assez grande?
12 La chambre, c'est combien?
13 La Peugeot est en panne?
14 Il y a un téléphone par ici?

Answer these questions with **non**. Use **je** and **ne pas**.

15 Vous avez une carte de crédit?
16 Vous êtes le garçon?
17 Avez-vous une autre question?

Now give your own answers. Don't worry if mine are different.

18 Où allez-vous?
19 A quelle heure désirez-vous manger?
20 Où est l'hôtel La Belle Provence?

Answers

1 Vous avez une chambre pour deux?
2 Vous avez l'addition, s'il vous plaît?/ Avez-vous…?
3 C'est à quelle heure le petit déjeuner?
4 Le téléphone est en panne.
5 Peut-il le réparer?
6 Nous voudrions manger quelque chose.
7 Où est le café, à gauche ou à droite?
8 C'est combien?
9 Nous le/la prenons.
10 Je travaille de neuf heures à six heures.

11 Oui, la chambre est assez grande.
12 La chambre est à deux cents francs.
13 Oui, la Peugeot est en panne.
14 Oui, il y a un téléphone par ici.
15 Non, je n'ai pas une carte de crédit.
16 Non, je ne suis pas le garçon.
17 Non, je n'ai pas une autre question.
18 Nous allons à Paris.
19 Nous voudrions manger à huit heures.
20 L'hôtel La Belle Provence est en Provence.

▶ Learn by heart

Learn the following lines by heart. When you know them say them fast and with a bit of drama. Put the name of a friend after **avec**.

Je n'ai pas beaucoup d'argent, mais...

Je n'ai pas beaucoup d'argent,
mais je voudrais aller en vacances avec ...
Nous voudrions aller à St Tropez en Renault.
Il y a beaucoup de petits hôtels pas chers.
Malheureusement ce n'est pas possible.
Il y a toujours trop de travail à mon bureau
et ... la Renault est en panne!

Test your progress

Translate in writing. What do you remember without checking back?

1 We would like to have (take) a coffee.
2 Is there a bank around here?
3 We are going to eat something.
4 Do you have the bill for the tea, please?
5 My children do not have enough (of) money.
6 At what time are we in the office?
7 They always go to the café at half past six.
8 Another question please: where are the toilets, straight ahead?
9 You are going to Oslo in January?
10 She goes to Los Angeles with her husband.
11 The breakfast is great. How much is it?
12 Where are you tomorrow at half past ten?
13 There is no job without a computer.
14 I am going to the office and then on holiday.
15 Excuse me, we only have a credit card.
16 All right, we'll take the Renault for two days.
17 We are going to repair the Citroën. It is broken.
18 I work 12 hours. We need money.
19 Fifteen francs for a cold tea. That's too much.
20 There are 300 cafés around here, one at two minutes from here.

The answers are on page 75. The Progress chart awaits your score!

03
week three

Study for 35 minutes a day – but there are no penalties for doing more!

Day one

- Read **We are going shopping**.
- Listen to/Read **Nous allons faire les courses**.
- Read the **New words**, then learn some of them.

Day two

- Repeat the story and **New words**.
- Learn all the **New words**. Use the **Flash words!**

Day three

- Test yourself on all the **New words** – Boring, boring, but you are over half way already!
- Have a first look at **Learn by heart**.
- Learn the **Good news grammar**.

Day four

- Cut out and learn the **Flash sentences**.
- Listen to/Read **Learn by heart**.

Day five

- Listen to/Read **Let's speak French**.
- Listen to/Read **Spot the keys**.

Day six

- Have a quick look at the **New words** Weeks 1–3.
  You know 218 words by now! ... well, more or less.
- Translate: **Test your progress**.

Day seven: Enjoy your day off!

day-by-day guide

We are going shopping

Tom and Kate have rented a holiday apartment just outside Nice. Kate plans some shopping.

Kate   Today we must do the shopping. We are going to take the bus for the town centre.

Tom   But the weather is bad. It makes cold and there is sport on the television ... golf at one o'clock and a half.

Kate   I am sorry but we must first go to the cash dispenser of the bank, then to the post office to buy stamps and afterwards to the chemist's and to the dry cleaner's.

Tom   Well, no golf ... perhaps football at three o'clock. That is all for the shopping?

Kate   No, I must go in a department store, to the supermarket and to the hairdresser. And afterwards in a shoe-shop.

Tom   My God! The shops are open until what hour?

Kate   Until 7 o'clock, I believe.

Tom   Well, no football ... but perhaps tennis at seven o'clock and quarter.

(Later)

Kate   I believe that I have bought too many things: bread, a half kilo of cheese, 200 grams of ham, potatoes, butter, eggs, sugar, six bottles of beer and a bottle of wine.

Tom   That's all right. No problem. We have enough for tomorrow. We have not much eaten yesterday. What is it that this is? What is it that there is in the big bag? Is it for me?

Kate   Well, I was at the hairdresser's at Galeries Lafayette and I have seen shoes exactly at my size. They are super, no? Blue with white. The sales assistant was very nice and gorgeous, like Tom Cruise.

Tom   Who is Tom Cruise? And how much the shoes?

Kate   They were a little expensive, but the same price as in England ... 900 francs.

Tom   What? But this is a price mad!

Kate   But this t-shirt of golf was very cheap, in size 44, only 85 francs, and I have bought a newspaper English and ... is there not tennis on the television now?

▶ Nous allons faire les courses

Tom and Kate have rented a holiday apartment just outside Nice. Kate plans some shopping.

Kate   Aujourd'hui nous devons faire des courses. Nous allons prendre le bus pour le centre ville.

Tom   Mais le temps est mauvais. Il fait froid et il y a du sport à la télé ... du golf, à une heure et demie.

Kate   Je suis désolée mais nous devons d'abord aller au distributeur de la banque, ensuite à la poste acheter des timbres et après, à la pharmacie et au pressing.

Tom   Alors, pas de golf ... peut-être du football à trois heures. C'est tout pour les courses?

Kate   Non, je dois aller dans un grand magasin, au supermarché et chez le coiffeur. Et après, dans un magasin de chaussures.

Tom   Mon Dieu! Les magasins sont ouverts jusqu'à quelle heure?

Kate   Jusqu'à sept heures, je crois.

Tom   Alors, pas de football ... mais peut-être du tennis à sept heures et quart.

(Plus tard)

Kate   Je crois que j'ai acheté trop de choses: du pain, un demi kilo de fromage, 200 grammes de jambon, des pommes de terre, du beurre, des oeufs, du sucre, six bouteilles de bière et une bouteille de vin.

Tom   C'est bien. Pas de problème. Nous avons assez pour demain. Nous n'avons pas beaucoup mangé hier. Qu'est-ce que c'est? Qu'est-ce qu'il y a dans le grand sac? C'est pour moi?

Kate   Alors, j'étais chez le coiffeur aux Galeries Lafayette et j'ai vu des chaussures exactement à ma taille. Elles sont superbes, non? Du bleu avec du blanc. Le vendeur était très sympathique et adorable comme Tom Cruise.

Tom   Qui est Tom Cruise? Et combien les chaussures?

Kate   Elles étaient un peu chères, mais le même prix qu'en Angleterre ... neuf cents francs.

Tom   Quoi? Mais c'est un prix fou!

Kate   Mais ce tee-shirt de golf était très bon marché, en taille quarante-quatre, seulement quatre-vingt cinq francs, et j'ai acheté un journal anglais et ... il n'y a pas de tennis à la télé maintenant?

New words

Learn the **New words** in half the time by using the **Flash cards**. There are 18 to start you off. Get a friend to make the rest!

faire *(to) do, make*
faire les courses *(to) do the shopping*
aujourd'hui *today*
nous devons *we must*
le bus *the bus*
le centre ville *the town / city centre*
le temps *the weather*
mauvais(e) *bad*
il fait froid *it is cold* (lit. *it makes cold*)
la télé(vision) *the TV*
je suis désolé(e) *I am sorry*
d'abord *first*
le distributeur (automatique) *the cash dispenser*
la poste *the post office*
acheter *(to) buy*
les timbres *the stamps*
après *afterwards, later*
la pharmacie *the chemist's*
le pressing *the dry cleaner's*
alors *so, then*
tout(e) *all*
je dois *I must*
le grand magasin *the department store*
le supermarché *the supermarket*
le coiffeur *the hairdresser*
le magasin *the shop*
les chaussures *the shoes*
Mon Dieu! *My God!*
ouvert(e) *open*
jusqu'à *until*
je crois *I believe*
plus *more*
plus tard *later*

j'ai acheté *I have bought, I bought*
les choses *the things*
le pain *the bread*
un demi kilo *half a kilo*
le fromage *the cheese*
le jambon *the ham*
les pommes de terre *the potatoes*
le beurre *the butter*
les oeufs *the eggs*
le sucre *the sugar*
la bouteille *the bottle*
la bière *the beer*
le vin *the wine*
c'est bien *that's all right*
pas de problème *no problem*
nous avons mangé *we have eaten, we ate*
hier *yesterday*
qu'est-ce que...? *what* (lit. *what is it that*)...?
le sac *the bag*
moi *me*
Galeries Lafayette *a well-known French chain of department stores*
j'ai vu *I have seen, I saw*
exactement *exactly*
à ma taille *in my size*
bleu(e) *blue*
blanc, blanche *white*
le vendeur *the sales assistant*
il était, ils étaient *he was, they were*
sympathique *nice, pleasant*
comme *like, also: how*
qui *who*

le, la même... que *the same... as*	**ce, cette** *this*
le prix *the price*	**bon marché** *cheap*
Angleterre *England*	**le journal** *the newspaper*
quoi *what*	**anglais(e)** *English*
fou, folle *mad, crazy*	**maintenant** *now*

TOTAL NEW WORDS: 74
...only 159 words to go!

▶ Some easy extras

Les couleurs (the colours)

blanc, blanche *white*
noir, noire *black*
rouge *red*
bleu, bleue *blue*
vert, verte *green*
jaune *yellow*
brun, brune, marron *brown*
gris, grise *grey*
orange *orange*
rose *pink*

Spend 5 minutes learning **devoir**:

devoir *must*	
je dois	*I must*
vous devez	*you must*
nous devons	*we must*
il doit	*he, it must*
elle doit	*she, it must*
ills/elles doivent	*they must*

▶ Learn by heart

Say these seven lines in under a minute! The more expression you use the easier it will be to remember all the useful bits later.

Pas de problème!

Aujourd'hui nous devons faire les courses – pas de problème!
Alors, nous prenons le bus pour le centre ville.
Mon Dieu! Je crois que je n'ai pas assez d'argent.
Où y a-t-il un distributeur?
Je suis désolée, j'ai trop acheté: du pain, du beurre, du jambon et du fromage, et cinq bouteilles de vin rouge...
Mais le vendeur était adorable!

Good news grammar

1 The past.   Quite straight forward!

When you talk about something that happened before, or in the past, in French you usually use **avoir** plus the other verb, slightly changed. Remember **travailler**, a regular fellow, with nice regular endings? If you want to say in French that you *have worked*, or that *you worked*, you would say **j'ai travaillé**. If you *have bought* something you would say **j'ai acheté**, and if someone *repaired* something, you would say **il a reparé**. Every time, the ending of the main verb changes to –é.

Unfortunately some verbs have their very own words for the past.

For example: **prendre** becomes **pris** (*taken*) and **faire** becomes **fait** (*made, done*). When you learn your **New words** in Weeks 4, 5 and 6, you'll often find the past next to it like this: **je connais/connu** *I know/known*. You can then 'mix and match' by yourself:

Je **connais** Yvette. Nous avons **connu** Pierre.

There's a list of all **Instant** verbs in Week 6. Have a sneak preview!

2 *Aller à, aller dans, aller chez:* going to …

No need to stamp your foot. You can use **à** most of the time. If you are going to an office or a shop and use **à**, it would be a quick pit-stop. When you use **dans**, it means that you are spending time inside, like in a store. And you use **chez** when you are calling on a particular person there.

Remember Kate? She went to the post office, the department store and the hairdresser's: **à** la poste, **dans** un grand magasin and **chez** le coiffeur. But if you muddle them up there are no penalties!

3 *Qu'est-ce que c'est:* What's this? What's that? What is it?

Word by word it means *what is it that it is?* Talk about making a meal of it! When a French person asks this, it sounds like 'case-ke-say?' Say it fast and use it!

4 *Qu'est-ce qu'il y a?:* What is there? What is the matter?

Word by word it means *What is it that there is?* Say it fast 'case-keelia?' and use it!

5 *Vin rouge, journal anglais*

Except for such frequently used words as **grand**, **petit** or **bon**, adjectives usually follow the noun. So it's *wine red* and *newspaper English*.

▶ Let's speak French

Over to you! If you have the recording, use it to check your answers.

Let's start with a ten point warm up. Say in French:

1 We need 300 francs.
2 We must go to the bank.
3 Who is (it) on the T.V.?
4 Is there a sales assistant here?
5 Are the shops open?
6 They were here from 6 to 10.
7 I must buy something.
8 Is there a bus for the centre?
9 My God, it is cold today!
10 It's too expensive. I'm sorry.

Answer in French using **non** and **nous**:

11 Vous avez vu le football?
12 Vous avez mangé le pâté?
13 Vous avez acheté le journal?
14 Vous avez vu le golf?
15 Vous avez acheté beaucoup de bière?

Now ask some questions in French starting with **qu'est-ce que**. Then answer in French using the word in brackets:

16	What is this?	(my beer)
17	What is there?	(the drycleaner's)
18	What did you buy?	(a newspaper)
19	What did you see?	(golf on T.V.)
20	What did you eat?	(a lot of cheese)

Answers

1 Nous avons besoin de trois cent francs.
2 Nous devons aller à la banque.
3 Qui c'est à la télé?
4 Il y a un vendeur par ici?
5 Les magasins sont ouverts?
6 Ils étaient ici de six heures à dix heures.
7 Je dois acheter quelque chose.
8 Y a-t-il un bus pour le centre ville?
9 Mon Dieu, aujourd'hui il fait froid!
10 C'est trop cher. Je suis désolé.
11 Non, nous n'avons pas vu le football.
12 Non, nous n'avons pas mangé le pâté.

13 Non, nous n'avons pas acheté le journal.
14 Non, nous n'avons pas vu le golf.
15 Non, nous n'avons pas acheté beaucoup de bière.
16 Qu'est-ce que c'est? C'est ma bière.
17 Qu'est-ce qu'il y a? C'est le pressing.
18 Qu'est-ce que vous avez acheté? J'ai/nous avons acheté un journal.
19 Qu'est-ce que vous avez vu? J'ai/nous avons vu du golf à la télé.
20 Qu'est-ce que vous avez mangé? J'ai/nous avons mangé beaucoup de fromage.

▶ Spot the keys

By now you can say many things in French. But what happens if you ask a question and do not understand the answer – hitting you at the speed of an automatic rifle? No need to panic. Listen for familiar words – **key words** which tell you what the other person is saying.

If you have the recording, listen to the dialogue, if you don't – read on.

You: **Excusez moi, où est la poste?**

Answer: *Alors, c'est* *très* *simple. D'abord* **tout droit jusqu'** *au prochain* *croisement,* *là-bas* *près* *de la* **maison rouge. Ensuite à gauche, il y a** *une résidence du troisième âge et tout une rangée de* **magasins.** *Et immédiatement* *après un* **pressing à droite,** *vous* *arrivez* *sur le* **parking de la place de la poste.**

Can you find your way with the key words? I think you'll get there!

Test your progress

Translate in writing. Then check the answers and be amazed!

1 Have you seen a sales assistant?
2 At what time must you go to the office today?
3 Who saw Pierre on the television yesterday?
4 I believe that the shops are open now.
5 Is there a department store around here or in the centre?
6 Excuse me, I must go to the post office. You, too?
7 Where did you buy the English newspaper?
8 The weather is bad today? It is cold.
9 What? Is that all? That was very cheap!
10 A stamp for (the) England – it is how much?
11 I have a credit card. Is there a cash dispenser?
12 We must go to the dry cleaner's. That's all right, no problem.
13 Do you have a bag for my black shoes please?
14 I believe I have seen a chemist's around here.
15 Size 12 English – that is what in France?
16 Did you work until 5 o'clock or later?
17 I am sorry, we have eaten all the ham.
18 First I must repair the bag, and then we can do the shopping.
19 We have taken everything: beer, wine and cheese.
20 That was a very nice sales assistant.

Remember to fill in the Progress chart! You are now halfway home.

04

week four

Study 35 minutes a day but if you are keen try 40... 45...!

Day one

- Read **We are going to have dinner**.
- Listen to/Read **Nous allons dîner**.
- Read the **New words**. Learn the easy ones.

Day two

- Repeat the dialogue. Learn the harder **New words**.
- Cut out the **Flash words** to help you.

Day three

- Learn all the **New words** until you know them well.
- Read and learn the **Good news grammar**.

Day four

- Cut out and learn the **Flash sentences**.
- Listen to/Read **Learn by heart**.

Day five

- Listen to/Read **Let's speak French**.
- Read **Say it simply**.

Day six

- Listen to/Read **Spot the keys**.
- Translate **Test your progress**.

Day seven

Are you keeping your scores above 60%? In that case ... **have a good day off!**

We are going to eat out

Tom and Kate are still in Nice. Alain Durant is inviting them to dinner.

Kate   Somebody has telephoned. He didn't say why. The name and the number are on this paper. Mr Durant from Lyon.

Tom   Ah yes, Alain Durant, a very good client of the company. I know him well. He is very nice. I have an appointment with him on Thursday. It is a very important matter.
(On the telephone.) Hello? Good morning Mr Durant. This is Tom Walker. How are you? Yes, thank you ... Yes, sure, that is possible ... next week ... yes, very interesting ... pardon? ... no we have time ... super ... no, only some days ... oh yes!... when? ... at eight o'clock ... upstairs, at the exit ... in front of the door. Well, until this evening. Thank you very much and goodbye.

Kate   What are we doing this evening?

Tom   We are going to have dinner with Mr Durant. In the centre, behind the church. He says that the restaurant is new and very good. Mr Durant is in Nice for two days with Edith and Peter Palmer from the office.

Kate   I know Edith Palmer. I do not like her. She is very snobbish and has a horrible dog. I believe I am going to be ill. 'Flu' with headaches. Where is the number of the doctor...?

Tom   No, that's not possible. Mr Durant is very nice. One cannot do that.

(In the restaurant Léon, the waiter, explains the menu.)

Léon   We have menus at 120 francs or at 160 francs or à la carte. The dessert of the day is chocolate mousse with ice cream or cream.

Alain   Mrs Walker, can I help you? Perhaps a soup and fish or meat?

Kate   A steak with salad, please.

Edith   Too much red meat, it's not good for you, Kate.

Alain   And for you, Mr. Walker? What would you like to drink?

Tom   Now then, I would like an escalope in cream sauce and some red wine, please.

Edith   Tom, there is a lot of cream, that is too much for you.

····➤ Page 46

▶ Nous allons dîner

Tom and Kate are still in Nice. Alain Durant is inviting them to dinner.

Kate Quelqu'un a téléphoné. Il n'a pas dit pourquoi. Le nom et le numéro sont sur ce papier. Monsieur Durant de Lyon.

Tom Ah oui, Alain Durant ! Un très bon client du bureau. Je le connais bien. Il est très sympathique. J'ai rendez-vous avec lui jeudi. C'est une affaire très importante. *(Au téléphone.)* Allô! Bonjour, Monsieur Durant. Ici Tom Walker. Ça va? Oui, merci ... Oui, bien sûr, c'est possible ... la semaine prochaine ... oui, très intéressant ... pardon ? ... non, nous avons le temps ... superbe ... non, seulement quelques jours ...ah oui! ... quand? ... à huit heures ... en haut, à la sortie ... devant la porte. Alors, à ce soir. Merci beaucoup et au revoir.

Kate Que faisons-nous ce soir?

Tom Nous allons dîner avec Monsieur Durant. Dans le centre, derrière l'église. Il dit que le restaurant est nouveau et très bon. Monsieur Durant est à Nice pour deux jours avec Edith et Peter Palmer du bureau.

Kate Je connais Edith Palmer. Je ne l'aime pas. Elle est très snob et a un chien horrible! Je crois que je vais être malade. Une grippe avec des maux de tête. Où est le numéro du médecin ...?

Tom Non, ce n'est pas possible! Monsieur Durant est très sympathique. On ne peut pas faire ça.

(Le garçon, Léon, explique le menu.)

Léon Nous avons des menus à cent vingt francs ou cent soixante francs ou à la carte. Le dessert du jour, c'est de la mousse au chocolat avec de la glace ou de la crème fraîche.

Alain Madame Walker, puis-je vous aider? Peut-être un potage et un poisson ou une viande?

Kate Un steak avec de la salade, s'il vous plaît.

Edith Trop de viande rouge, ce n'est pas bon pour vous, Kate.

Alain Et pour vous, Monsieur Walker? Que désirez-vous boire?

Tom Alors, je voudrais une escalope à la crème et du vin rouge, s'il vous plaît.

Edith Tom, il y a beaucoup de crème. C'est trop pour vous.

······▶ Page 47

Alain	And you, Mrs. Palmer?
Edith	A little grilled chicken, vegetables and a glass of water, please.

(Later)

Alain	Has everyone finished? Would you like some fruit, some cheese, some coffee? No, nothing? Nobody? Well then, the bill please.
Edith	Oh, Monsieur Durant, can you help me please? How do you say 'doggie bag' in French? I would like a plastic bag for my dog.
Kate	But Edith, the dog is in England!

New words

dîner/dîné *to eat out, dine/eaten out, dined*
quelqu'un *someone*
il a téléphoné *he has telephoned*
il a dit *he has said/said*
pourquoi *why*
le numéro *the number*
sur *on*
le papier *the paper*
un client *a client*
le *(on its own)* *him, it*
je connais/connu *I know/known*
bien *well*
(le) rendez-vous *the meeting*
lui *him*
jeudi *Thursday*
une affaire *a matter*
important(e) *important*
ça va? *how are you?*
bien sûr *sure, of course*
possible *possible*
prochain(e) *next*
nous avons le temps *we have time*
quelques jours *a few days*
quand *when*

en haut *above, upstairs*
la sortie *the exit*
devant *in front of*
la porte *the door*
mardi *Tuesday*
merci, merci bien *thank you*
merci beaucoup *thank you very much*
nous faisons/fait *we do, make/done, made*
derrière *behind*
l'église *the church*
il dit *he says*
nouveau, nouvelle *new*
j'aime *I like, love*
snob *snob, snobbish*
un chien *a dog*
horrible *horrible*
malade *ill, sick*
une grippe *flu*
les maux de tête *headaches*
le médecin *the doctor*
le menu *the menu*
le dessert du jour *the dessert of the day*
la mousse au chocolat *the chocolate mousse*
la glace *the ice cream*

Alain	Et vous, Madame Palmer?
Edith	Un peu de poulet grillé, des légumes et un verre d'eau, s'il vous plaît.

(Plus tard)

Alain	Tout le monde a terminé? Vous désirez des fruits, du fromage, du café? Non, rien? Personne? Bien, alors l'addition s'il vous plaît.
Edith	Ah, Monsieur Durant, vous pouvez m'aider, s'il vous plaît? Comment dit-on 'doggy bag' en français? Je voudrais un sac plastique pour mon chien.
Kate	Mais Edith, le chien est en Angleterre!!

je peux, *but:* **puis-je?** *I can, can I?*
aider/aidé *(to) help/helped*
un potage *a soup*
un poisson *a fish*
une viande *a meat*
la salade *the salad*
boire *(to) drink*
alors *now then, well*
le poulet grillé *the grilled chicken*
les légumes *the vegetables*
un verre d'eau *a glass of water*

tout le monde *everyone*
terminé(e) *finished*
les fruits *the fruit*
rien *nothing*
personne *nobody*
vous pouvez m'aider? *can you help me?*
on *one (as in: one should not...)*
comment dit-on? *how does one say?*
en français *in French*
en plastique *plastic*

TOTAL NEW WORDS: 69
...only 90 words to go!

▶ Last easy extras

les jours de la semaine (days of the week)

lundi	*Monday*	**vendredi**	*Friday*
mardi	*Tuesday*	**samedi**	*Saturday*
mercredi	*Wednesday*	**dimanche**	*Sunday*
jeudi	*Thursday*		

Good news grammar

1 The future – easy!

If you want to talk about something that *is going* to happen –
later, tomorrow, in the future – you can use **aller**:

Nous **allons** faire les courses. *We are going to do the shopping.*

Je **vais** acheter un ordinateur. *I am going to buy a computer.*

Vous **allez** être malade, Kate? *Are you going to be ill, Kate?*

2 *le, la, les:* him, her, it, them

Imagine you are talking about people or things, let's say about
somebody or something you know and must see – Pierre,
Louise, a shop, the TV or the photos. If you want to say: *him,
her, it* or *them,* in French you use: **le, la** or **les**. There is no
special word for *it*.

Pierre? Je **le** connais, je dois **le** voir.

Louise? Je **la** connais, je dois **la** voir.

le magasin? Je **le** connais, je dois **le** voir.

la télé? Je **la** connais, je dois **la** voir.

les photos? Je **les** connais, je dois **les** voir.

Notice that **le, la** and **les** go right in front of the verb, if there is
just one: Je **le** connais. *I him know.*

If there are two verbs **le, la** or **les** go in front of the second one:
Je dois **le** voir. *I must him see.*

3 *Vous désirez? Je voudrais…* would like

When eating out the waiter or your host would normally ask:
Qu'est-ce que vous **désirez?** And you would answer: **Je
voudrais…**

(Not the other way around: Vous voudriez? Je désire…. Non,
non!)

Last two verb boxes: learn them NOW

vouloir – *want to*	
je voudrais	*I would like to*
vous voudriez	*you would like to*
nous voudrions	*we would like to*
il/elle voudrait	*he/she would like to*
ils/elles voudraient	*they would like to*

pouvoir – *can*	
je peux	*I can*
but: puis-je?	*can I*
vous pouvez	*you can*
nous pouvons	*we can*
il/elle peut	*he/she can*
ils/elles peuvent	*they can*

▶ Learn by heart

Pretend this is a telephone call by a rather opinionated person. When you have learned it by heart, try to act it out in 50 seconds.

Je suis très intéressant

Voudriez-vous dîner avec moi ce soir?

Je connais un très bon restaurant et le vin est superbe.

Non?

Pourquoi pas? Je suis très intéressant.

Vous ne me connaissez pas?

Mais bien sûr. Vous me voyez beaucoup à la télé.

La météo* – c'est moi!

Vous ne pouvez pas? Pourquoi pas?

Vous avez un rendez-vous important?

Oh, non! Ce n'est pas possible!

French weather forecast

If you are short of time this week, you can settle for the slightly shorter piece which follows... or you could do both!

Je ne l'aime pas

Vous connaissez Monsieur Dupont? Je dois aller dîner avec lui.

Pourquoi?

C'est un très bon client du bureau. Mais je ne l'aime pas. Il mange et il boit trop.

Et quand?

Ce soir! Il y a du football à la télé! Toujours le bureau!

Ah, je suis désolée!

This week's tip: *vous* or *tu*?

There are two ways of saying 'you' in French: **vous** or **tu**. Vous is formal and polite. When in France and speaking **Instant French** use **vous**. Tu is for family and friends, and needs a whole lot of extra grammar! Next year!

◖ Let's speak French

Here are ten sentences as a warm-up. Use the recording if you have it.

1 Who has telephoned and why?
2 He says that I know him.
3 I believe that we have (the) time later.
4 I do not like the chicken.
5 A glass of red wine please.
6 Yes, sure, I have an appointment with you.
7 Everybody is on holiday.
8 He said that it is all right.
9 I can go next week with him.
10 Does somebody have the number?

Now pretend you are in France with friends who do not speak French. They want you to ask people things in French. They say: **Please ask him…**

11 if he can help the client
12 if he phoned yesterday
13 why he has bought the Ferrari
14 if he has (an) appointment today
15 where one can buy a newspaper

On another occasion they will ask you to **tell** people things. They will say: **Please tell her…** If you don't know the odd word use your **Instant** words.

16 that the soup is cold
17 that I am a vegetarian
18 that we don't have his number
19 that we are unfortunately in a rush now
20 that next week will suit us

Answers

1 Qui a téléphoné et pourquoi?
2 Il dit que je le connais.
3 Je crois que nous avons le temps plus tard.
4 Je n'aime pas le poulet.
5 Un verre de vin rouge, s'il vous plaît.
6 Oui, bien sûr, j'ai un rendez-vous avec vous.
7 Tout le monde est en vacances.
8 Il a dit que c'est bien.
9 Je peux aller avec lui la semaine prochaine.
10 Quelqu'un a le numéro?

11 Vous pouvez aider le client?
12 Vous avez téléphoné hier?
13 Pourquoi avez-vous acheté la Ferrari?
14 Vous avez rendez-vous aujourd'hui?
15 Où peut-on acheter un journal?
16 Excusez moi mais le potage est froid.
17 Il/elle ne mange pas de viande.
18 Nous n'avons pas son numéro.
19 Malheureusement nous n'avons pas le temps maintenant.
20 C'est bien, la semaine prochaine.

Say it simply

When people want to speak French but don't dare, it's usually because they are trying to *translate* what they want to say from English into French. But because they don't know some of the words, they give up!

With **Instant French**, you work around the words you don't know with the words you know. And believe me, 378 words are enough to say anything! It may not always be very elegant – but that's not the point. You are speaking, *communicating*!

Here are three examples showing you how to say things in a simple way. I have highlighted the English words which are not part of the **Instant** vocabulary.

1 In English:

You need to **change** your **flight** to London from Tuesday to Friday.

Saying it simply:

> **'Nous ne pouvons pas aller à Londres mardi, nous voudrions aller à Londres vendredi.'**
>
> or: **'Mardi n'est pas bon pour nous. Nous voudrions prendre l'avion vendredi.'**

2 In English:

You want to get your **purse** and **mobile phone** from the coach which the driver has locked.

Saying it simply:

> **'J'ai besoin de mon argent et de mon petit téléphone. Ils sont dans le bus mais le bus n'est pas ouvert.'**

3 This time your friend has just cracked the heel of her only pair of shoes. You have to catch a train soon and need some instant help. This is what you could simply say:

> **'Excusez-moi, nous avons un problème avec une chaussure. Il y a un magasin par ici où on peut la réparer – maintenant?'**

▶ Spot the keys

You practised listening for key words when you asked the way to the post office in Week 3. Now you are in a department store and ask the sales assistant if the black shoes you fancy are also available in size 39. She says 'non', then 'un moment, s'il vous plaît' and disappears. When she comes back this is what she says:

J'ai téléphoné ànotrecentrale mais illeurreste ce modèle de **chaussures seulement** *en* **bleu**. *Maisnousenavonsen* **noir** *en* **trente-huit** *et je sais par expérience que ce modèle chausse normalement* **très grand**. *Àmonavis elles seront* **assez grandes**.

Size 39 was only available in blue but size 38 might be big enough.

Test your progress

Translate into French:
1 Sure, the appointment was Wednesday, at the office.
2 Next week? No, that's not possible. We don't have (the) time.
3 I would like a glass of champagne and then a bottle of white wine.
4 Can you help me, please. Someone needs the number of the doctor.
5 He said that the church is very interesting. Have you seen it?
6 We would like to eat with you Monday night.
7 Where can one buy fruit and vegetables around here?
8 The cash dispenser is upstairs, in front of the exit.
9 We'll take the chicken or the ham salad. The fish is too expensive.
10 I know the wines of Bordeaux well. They are superb.
11 On Friday we are going to the client. It is a very important matter.
12 I would like to buy something. How do you say in French...?
13 I do not like the Mercedes. I am going to take the small Peugeot.
14 He says that he has the flu and that he has not finished the work.
15 Everybody has phoned this evening. It's crazy!
16 Who saw that the dog has eaten my meat?
17 There is ice cream. But I do not like chocolate ice cream.
18 How are you? You are sick? You must drink a lot of water.
19 When are we going this week to Lyon and why?
20 What are we doing in this hotel? It is horrible.

How are your 'shares' looking on the Progress chart? Going up?

05
week five

How about 15 minutes on the train / tube / bus, 10 minutes on the way home and 20 minutes before switching on the television...?

Day one

- Read **On the move**.
- Listen to/Read **En route**.
- Read the **New words**. Learn 15 or more.

Day two

- Repeat **En route** and the **New words**.
- Cut out the **Flash words** and get stuck in.

Day three

- Test yourself to perfection on all the **New words**.
- Listen to/Read **Learn by heart**.

Day four

- Cut out and learn the **Flash sentences**.
- Read and learn the **Good news grammar**.

Day five

- Listen to/Read **Let's speak French**.

Day six

- Listen to/Read **Spot the keys**.
- Translate **Test your progress**.

Day seven

**How is the Progress chart looking? Great?... Great!
I bet you don't want a day off ... but I insist!**

On the move

Tom and Kate are now travelling along the Côte d'Azur, by train, bus and hire car. They talk to Renée, the ticket clerk at the station, to Jim in the train and later to Luc, the bus driver.

(At the station)

Tom   Two tickets to Cannes, please.

Renée   Return tickets?

Tom   What? Can you please speak more slowly.

Renée   Return – tickets?

Tom   One way please. At what time does the train leave, and from where?

Renée   At nine forty-five, platform eight.

Kate   Tom, quickly, here are two non-smoking seats. Oh, somebody is smoking over there. Excuse me, it is forbidden to smoke because it is non-smoking here.

Jim   Sorry, I don't understand, I come from England.

(At the bus stop)

Kate   The next bus for Nice is at six o'clock. We have to wait ten minutes. Tom, here are my postcards and a letter. There is a letterbox down below. I am going to take some photos over there. The coast is superb in the sun.

Tom   Kate, quickly, here are two blue buses. This one is full, let's take the other one. *(In the bus.)* Two tickets for Nice, please.

Luc   This bus goes only to Cannes.

Tom   But we are in Cannes.

Luc   Yes, yes, but the bus goes to the Cannes hospital.

(In the car)

Tom   Here is our car. Only 400 francs for three days. I am very pleased.

Kate   I do not like this car. It was not expensive because it is old. I hope that we are not going to have problems.

Tom   I am sorry, but the first car was too expensive and the second one too big. This one was the last.

           (Later) Where are we? Where is the map? On the left there is a service station and on the right a school. Quickly!

⸱⸱⸱⸱▶ Page 58

▶ En route

Tom and Kate are now travelling along the Côte d'Azur by train, bus and hired car. They talk to Renée, the ticket clerk at the station, to Jim in the train and later to Luc, the bus driver.

(À la gare)

Tom   Deux billets pour Cannes, s'il vous plaît.

Renée   Allerretour?

Tom   Comment? Pouvez-vous parler plus lentement, s'il vous plaît?

Renée   Aller – retour.

Tom   Aller simple, s'il vous plaît. À quelle heure part le train, et d'où?

Renée   À neuf heures quarante cinq, quai huit.

Kate   Tom, vite, ici il y a deux places pour non-fumeurs. Oh, quelqu'un fume là-bas. Excusez-moi, c'est interdit de fumer parce que c'est non-fumeur ici.

Jim   Sorry, je ne comprends pas. Je viens from England.

(À l'arrêt de bus)

Kate   Le prochain bus pour Nice est à six heures. Nous devons attendre dix minutes. Tom, voilà mes cartes postales et une lettre. Il y a une boîte aux lettres en bas. Je vais prendre des photos là-bas. La côte est superbe au soleil.

Tom   Kate, vite, voilà deux bus bleus. Celui-ci est plein. Prenons l'autre. *(Dans le bus.)* Deux billets pour Nice, s'il vous plaît.

Luc   Ce bus va seulement à Cannes.

Tom   Mais nous sommes à Cannes.

Luc   Oui, oui, mais le bus va jusqu'à l'hôpital de Cannes.

(Dans la voiture)

Tom   Voilà notre voiture. Seulement 400 francs pour trois jours. Je suis très content.

Kate   Je n'aime pas cette voiture. Elle n'était pas chère parce qu'elle est vieille. J'espère que nous n'allons pas avoir de problèmes.

Tom   Je suis désolé mais la première voiture était trop chère et la deuxième trop grande. Celle-ci était la dernière.

            (Plus tard) Où sommes-nous? Où est la carte? À gauche, il y a une station-service et à droite, une école. Vite!

••••▶ Page 59

Kate We are coming from the underground station. The main road is over there, next to the traffic light. If we go to the end we are on the motorway. In three kilometres. *(On the motorway.)* Why is this car very slow? Do we have enough petrol? How many litres? Do we have enough oil? Is the engine too hot? I believe the car has broken down. Where is the mobile? Where is the number of the garage? Where is my bag?

Tom My God, Kate! All these questions! Here comes the rain. And why are the police behind us?

New words

en route *on the move*
la gare *the railway station*
le billet *the ticket*
aller-retour *return ticket,*
  lit. *go-back*
comment *how, what, pardon?*
parler/parlé *(to) speak/spoken*
lente, lentement *slow, slowly*
aller simple *one way (ticket)*
il part *he, it leaves*
le train *the train*
le quai *the platform*
vite *quick, quickly*
non-fumeur *non-smoking*
il fume *he smokes*
là-bas *over there*
interdit *forbidden*
fumer/fumé *(to) smoke/smoked*
parce que *because*
je ne comprends pas *I do not*
  understand
je viens *I come*
l'arrêt (bus)/**la station** *the*
  stop, station
attendre/attendu *(to) wait/waited*
voilà *here is, there is*
la carte postale *the postcard*
la lettre *the letter*
la boîte *the box*

en bas *down below*
la photo *the photo*
la côte *the coast*
le soleil *the sun*
celui-ci, celle-ci *this one*
plein(e) *full*
l'hôpital *the hospital*
la voiture *the car*
notre *our*
content(e) *pleased*
vieux, vieille *old*
j'espère/espéré *I hope/hoped*
le premier, la première *the first*
le/la deuxième *the second*
le dernier, la dernière *the last*
la carte *the map*
la station-service *the petrol*
  station
l'école *the school*
nous venons *we come, are*
  coming
le métro *the metro (underground)*
la rue principale *the main road*
à côté de *next to, at the side*
  of
le feu rouge *the traffic light*
si *if*
le bout *the end*
l'autoroute *the motorway*

Kate   Nous venons de la station de métro. La rue principale est là-bas, à côté du feu rouge. Si nous allons jusqu'au bout, nous sommes sur l'autoroute. À trois kilomètres. *(Sur l'autoroute.)* Pourquoi cette voiture est-elle très lente? Avons-nous assez d'essence? Combien de litres? Avons-nous assez d'huile? Le moteur est trop chaud? Je crois que la voiture est en panne. Où est le téléphone portable? Où est le numéro du garage? Où est mon sac?

Tom   Mon Dieu, Kate! Toutes ces questions! Voilà la pluie! Et pourquoi la police est-elle derrière nous?

l'essence *the petrol*	**le téléphone portable** *the mobile phone*
le litre *the litre*	
l'huile *the oil*	**le garage** *the garage, workshop*
le moteur *the engine*	**la pluie** *the rain*
chaud(e) *hot*	**la police** *the police*

TOTAL NEW WORDS: 61
…only 29 words to go!

▶ Learn by heart

Someone has pranged the car and someone else is getting suspicious…! Try to say these lines fluently and like a prize-winning play!

Pouvons-nous aller au tennis?

Pouvons-nous aller au tennis?
Quelqu'un du bureau m'a donné deux billets.
Je voudrais voir le match des Américains.
Nous pouvons prendre le bus, le métro ou le train.

Le bus? le métro? le train? Pourquoi? Qu'est-ce qu'il y a?
Nous avons une bonne voiture en bas.

Alors… il y avait de la pluie et je n'ai pas vu le feu rouge,
mais ce n'est rien …
et le garçon du garage était très sympathique!

Good news grammar

1 How to say: my, your, our, his, her, their...

...winning lottery ticket, or anything else that belongs to someone.

Here's a box of tricks worth more than just a fleeting glance. You will use these 12 words every day, and they are quite easy to remember. You have met them before. Take three minutes to revise them.

mon, ma, mes	votre, vos	notre, nos	son, sa, ses	leur, leurs
my	*your*	*our*	*his, her*	*their*

Imagine you want to say: *my newspaper*, *my car* or *my shoes*. As you can see, there are three choices. So which one to pick? It's **mon** journal, **ma** voiture and **mes** chaussures.

Can you see what happened? **mon** goes with **le** words, **ma** goes with **la** words and **mes** goes with **les** words of more than one thing.

Notre and **votre** and **leur** are easy: **notre église** *our church*, **votre école** *your school*, **leur maison** *their house*.

Use **nos**, **vos**, and **leurs** for more than one thing, all words that start with **les**: **nos vacances** *our holidays*, **vos parents** *your parents*, **leurs enfants** *their children*.

But what about **son travail**? Does this mean *his* or *her work*? Both! The same applies to **sa mère**, *his* or *her mother*, and **ses amis**, *his* or *her friends*!

If you get in a muddle and say 'son mère' and 'sa travail'...? Pas de problème! Amazingly it usually turns out all right.

2 Me, you, us, him, her, them

Is this winning lottery ticket, pay increase, boring book ... for *me*, *you* or *him*? Here's another revision box. Have a two-minute look.

pour...	moi	vous	nous	lui	elle	eux	elles
for...	*me*	*you*	*us*	*him*	*her*	*them*(m)	*them*(f)

These words work with **avec, sans, de, chez, devant** and **derrière**: avec nous, sans moi, chez vous, devant lui.

▶ Let's speak French

Here's your ten point warm up: I give you an answer and you ask me a question – as if you did not hear very well the words in CAPITALS. Example: Pierre est ICI. Question: Où est Pierre?

1 Le téléphone portable est DANS MON SAC.
2 L'AUTOROUTE est là-bas.
3 Le bus part DANS VINGT MINUTES.
4 TOM voudrait parler avec Monsieur Durant.
5 Un aller-retour pour Paris, c'est 200 FRANCS.
6 Je n'aime pas la maison PARCE QU'elle est très vielle.
7 Ils vont en Angleterre EN VOITURE.
8 Je n'ai pas vu LE FEU ROUGE.
9 NON, je n'aime pas le garage.
10 OUI, je suis content de l'école.

Now answer starting with **oui** and **nous**:

11 Vous avez la carte de l'autoroute?
12 Vous allez prendre ce bus?
13 Vous pouvez fumer dans le train?
14 Vous devez attendre vingt minutes?
15 Vous allez maintenant à la gare?
16 Vous aimez la côte?

Explain these words in **Instant French**:

17 kennels   18 teacher   19 out of work   20 to be broke

Answers

1 Où est le téléphone portable?
2 C'est quoi, là-bas?
3 Quand part le bus?
4 Qui voudrait parler avec M. Durant?
5 C'est combien un aller-retour pour Paris?
6 Pourquoi vous n'aimez pas la maison?
7 Comment vont-ils en Angleterre?
8 Qu'est-ce que vous n'avez pas vu?
9 Vous n'aimez pas le garage?
10 Êtes-vous content de l'école?
11 Oui, nous avons la carte de l'autoroute.
12 Oui, nous allons prendre ce bus.
13 Oui, nous pouvons fumer dans le train.
14 Oui, nous devons attendre vingt minutes.
15 Oui, nous allons maintenant à la gare.
16 Oui, nous aimons la côte.
17 Une maison pour les chiens quand nous sommes en vacances.
18 Le monsieur ou la dame qui travaille avec les enfants à l'école.
19 Quelqu'un qui ne travaille pas.
20 Nous n'avons pas d'argent. Pas un franc!

❏ Spot the keys

This time you plan a trip in the country. What about the weather? This is what you ask:

Excusez-moi, quel temps fait-il aujourd'hui?

Here's the answer:

Eh bien, **je ne suis pas sûr si** *le dernier bulletin* **météo à la télévision est correct**, *mais d'après eux le système de basse pression se déplace progressivement et ils disent qu'il fera encore* **chaud aujourd'hui,** *environ* **vingt-cinq** *degrés. Mais nous aurons probablement encore* **un peu de pluie ce soir**.

He doesn't seem to be sure. According to the TV, it will be warm today – 25°C – with a little rain in the evening.

Test your progress

1 At what time is the next bus?
2 How much does a return ticket cost?
3 What did you say? Can you speak more slowly, please?
4 I do not understand why petrol is cheaper in America.
5 It is forbidden to smoke in the underground.
6 Quickly, here is the train. Platform three.
7 This box is for (the) postcards? A yellow letterbox?
8 Hello, I am coming from Calais. Is that the garage?
9 I hope that this is not the last service station.
10 It is very hot this week. I would like a little rain.
11 She did not wait for the traffic light, and now she is in hospital.
12 We did not see much sun. I am not happy.
13 She talks and smokes too much on the motorway! I am going to take the train.
14 We are at the police (station) because somebody has taken our mobile phone.
15 The tickets are cheap if you buy them now.
16 I like your Ferrari. Was it very expensive?
17 There is a chemist's behind the main road, next to the bus stop.
18 How is the car? It is old but the engine is new.
19 I need two tickets. Are there non-smoking seats?
20 Excuse me, I do not know the town. Where is the station?

If you know all your words, you should score over 90%!

06

week six

This is your last week! Need I say more?

Day one

- Read **In the airport**.
- Listen to/Read **À l'aéroport**.
- Read the **New words**. There are only 29!

Day two

- Repeat **À l'aéroport** and learn all the **New words**.
- Work with the **Flash words** and **Flash sentences**.

Day three

- Test yourself on the **Flash sentences**.
- Listen to/Read **Learn by heart**.

Day four

- No more **Good news grammar!** Have a look at the summary.
- Read **Say it simply**.
- Listen to/Read **Spot the keys**.

Day five

- Listen to/Read **Let's speak French**.

Day six

- Your last **Test your progress!** Go for it!

Day seven

Congratulations!

You have successfully completed the course and can now speak

Instant French!

---

day-by-day guide

At the airport

Tom and Kate are now on their way home to Birmingham. After a stop-over in Paris they are in the departure lounge of Charles de Gaulle airport and meet an old friend.

Tom   We have to work on Monday. It's horrible! I would like to leave for Italy now, or take a plane for Hawaii. My office can wait and nobody would ever know where I am.

Kate   And what are the people in *my* office going to say? They wait two days and telephone my mother. She'll surely give them the number of our mobile. And then?

Tom   Yes, yes, I know. Well, perhaps a week at Christmas in the snow or on a boat to Portugal ... I'm going to buy a newspaper ... Kate! Here is Mr Cardin!

Henri   Hello! How are you! What are you doing here? Here is my wife, Nancy. Your holidays are over? Was it good?

Kate   The Provence was wonderful. We have seen a lot of things and have eaten much too much. We know the Côte d'Azur well now.

Henri   Well, next year the Loire? Or you must come to Toulouse. Mrs Walker, my wife would like to buy a book on computers. Can you go with her and help her? Mr Walker, can you give me the newspaper? Is there something about the football? We have a beer afterwards?

(At the kiosk of the airport)

Kate   I don't see anything here. And what I see I do not like. Are you also going to England?

Nancy   No, we are going to Bordeaux to Robert's mother. She often has our children during the holidays. A boy and three girls. We are going to take the train tomorrow. It is less expensive.

Kate   Your husband works for the Bank of France?

Nancy   Yes, his work is interesting but not very well paid. We have a small apartment and an old Citroën. There is a lot to repair. My parents are in Los Angeles and I have a girlfriend in Dallas. We write a lot of letters. I would like to go to Los Angeles or Dallas but it is too expensive.

⸺▶ Page 68

▶ À l'aéroport

Tom and Kate are now on their way home to Birmingham. At Charles de Gaulle airport they meet an old friend.

Tom   Nous devons travailler lundi. C'est horrible! Je voudrais partir en Italie maintenant ou prendre l'avion pour Hawaii. Mon bureau peut attendre et personne ne sait jamais où je suis.

Kate   Et que disent les gens dans *mon* bureau? Ils attendent deux jours et téléphonent à ma mère. Elle leur donne bien sûr le numéro de notre portable. Et après?

Tom   Oui, oui, je sais. Alors, peut-être une semaine à Noël à la neige ou sur un bateau au Portugal... Je vais acheter le journal ... Kate! Voici Monsieur Cardin!

Henri   Bonjour, ça va? Que faites-vous ici? Voici ma femme, Nancy. Vos vacances sont terminées? C'était bien?

Kate   La Provence était merveilleuse. Nous avons vu beaucoup de choses et beaucoup trop mangé. Nous connaissons bien la Côte d'Azur maintenant.

Henri   L'année prochaine, la Loire, alors? Ou vous devez venir à Toulouse. Madame Walker, ma femme voudrait acheter un livre sur les ordinateurs. Pouvez-vous aller avec elle et l'aider? Monsieur Walker, pouvez-vous me donner le journal? Il y a quelque chose sur le football? Nous prenons une bière après?

(Au kiosque de l'aéroport)

Kate   Je ne vois rien ici. Et ce que vois, je n'aime pas. Vous allez aussi en Angleterre?

Nancy   Non, nous allons à Bordeaux, chez la mère de Robert. Elle a souvent nos enfants pendant les vacances. Un garçon et trois filles. Nous prenons le train demain. C'est moins cher.

Kate   Votre mari travaille à la Banque de France?

Nancy   Oui, son travail est intéressant mais pas très bien payé. Nous avons un petit appartement et une vieille Citroën. Il y a beaucoup à réparer. Mes parents sont à Los Angeles et j'ai une amie à Dallas. Nous nous écrivons beaucoup de lettres. Je voudrais aller à Los Angeles ou Dallas mais c'est trop cher.

⸺▶ Page 69

Kate	But you have a beautiful house in St Tropez!
Nancy	A house at St Tropez? I do not know the Côte d'Azur. When we have holidays we go to Lille to friends.
Tom	Kate, quickly! We have a plane to catch. Goodbye! What is the matter, Kate? What did Mrs Cardin say?
Kate	Wait, Tom, wait!!

New words

l'aéroport *the airport*
partir *(to) leave*
il sait *he knows*
jamais *never, ever*
ils disent/dit *they say/said*
les gens *the people*
ils attendent/attendu *they wait/waited*
ils téléphonent *they phone*
la mère *the mother*
leur *them*
elle donne *she gives*
je sais *I know*
à Noël *at Christmas*
à la neige *in the snow*
un bateau *a boat*

voici *here is*
merveilleux (-euse) *wonderful*
nous connaissons *we know*
l'année *the (course of the) year*
venir *(to) come*
donner/donné *(to) give/given*
je vois/vu *I see/seen*
souvent *often*
pendant *during*
la fille *the girl*
l'appartement *the apartment*
nous écrivons/écrit *we write/written*
chez des amis *at/to friends*
attends!/attendez! *wait!*

TOTAL NEW WORDS: 29
TOTAL FRENCH WORDS LEARNED: 378
EXTRA WORDS: 77

GRAND TOTAL: 455

Kate	Mais vous avez une belle maison à St Tropez!
Nancy	Une maison à St Tropez? Je ne connais pas la Côte d'Azur! Quand nous avons des vacances, nous allons à Lille chez des amis.
Tom	Kate, vite! Nous avons un avion à prendre. Au revoir ! Qu'est-ce qu'il y a, Kate? Qu'est-ce que Madame Cardin a dit?
Kate	Attends, Tom, attends!

▶ Learn by heart

This is your last dialogue to learn by heart. Give it your best! You now have six prize-winning party pieces and – a large store of everyday sayings which will be very useful.

Au revoir...

Kate	Bonjour, Monsieur Durant, c'est Kate Walker, de l'aéroport Charles de Gaulle. Oui, malheureusement nos vacances sont terminées. Merci beaucoup pour mardi soir. Tom voudrait parler avec vous... au revoir!
Tom	Allô, Jacques! Quoi? Vous allez acheter les deux? Mon bureau a votre e-mail*? C'est merveilleux! Merci beaucoup! L'année prochaine? Je voudrais voir la Loire. Avec Edith Palmer? Mon Dieu, non, non! Nous devons prendre l'avion. Au revoir!

---

* the proper French word is **courrier électronique,** but everyone who uses *e-mail* will know the word

Tip of the Week:

Plus and **moins**

If you want to say that something is bigger, hotter or more beautiful you just add **plus:**

    plus grand(e), **plus** chaud(e), **plus** beau/belle

If you want to say that something is less expensive or less interesting, you use **moins:**

    moins cher/chère, **moins** intéressant(e). Easy!

Good news grammar

As promised, there is no new grammar in this lesson. However, at times you may get entangled in the various verb forms, so here is a summary of all the **Instant** verbs which appear in the six weeks. When you read through them, you'll realize how many you know!

verb	je	vous	nous	il/elle	ils/elles	the past
avoir	ai	avez	avons	a	ont	
	avais		avions	avait	avaient	
acheter						acheté
aider						aidé
aller	vais	allez	allons	va	vont	
attendre				attend	attendent	attendu
boire	bois		buvons	boit		
désirer		désirez				
devoir	dois	devez	devons	doit	doivent	
dîner						dîné
dire				dit	disent	dit
donner				donne		donné
connaître	connais	connaissez	connaissons	connaît	connaissent	connu
croire	crois	croyez	croyons	croit	croient	
écrire			écrivons	écrit		
esperer	espère		espérons			espéré
être	suis	êtes	sommes	est	sont	
	étais	étiez	étions	était	étaient	
faire	fais	faites	faisons	fait	font	fait
fumer	fume	fumez	fumons	fume	fument	fumé
manger	mange	mangez	mangeons	mange	mangent	mangé
parler	parle	parlez	parlons	parle	parlent	parlé
partir	pars	partez	partons	part	partent	
prendre	prends	prenez	prenons	prend	prennent	pris
pouvoir	peux	pouvez	pouvons	peut	peuvent	
réparer						réparé
téléphoner					téléphonent	téléphoné
travailler	travaille	travaillez	travaillions	travaille	travaillent	travaillé
savoir	sais	savez	savons	sait	savent	
venir	viens	venez	venons	vient	viennent	
voir	vois	voyez	voyons	voit	voient	vu
vouloir	voudrais	voudriez	voudrions	voudrait	voudraient	

You'll notice lots of gaps. These are the ones I don't think you need to bother with for now. If you are dead keen, you can always look them up in a serious French grammar.

Tip: To say *I went to*, use *I was in*: **J'étais à Paris.** *I was in Paris.* Easy!

Say it simply

1 You are asking the dry cleaner for a same day service since you are leaving tomorrow. You also explain that the stain may be red wine.

2 You are at the airport, about to catch your flight home when you realise that you have left some clothes behind in the room of your hotel. You phone the hotel's housekeeper to ask her to send the things on to you.

What would you say? Say it, then write it down. Then see page 78.

◘ Spot the keys

Here are two final practice rounds. If you have the recording, close the book now. Find the key words and try to get the gist of it. Then check on page 78.

You might ask a taxi driver:

Combien de temps pour aller à l'aéroport? Et c'est combien?

His answer:

Cela dépend quand vous y allez. Normalement, ça prend vingt minutes mais s'il y a beaucoup de circulation et le pont sur la rivière est bouché, ça prend trois quarts d'heure. Le prix est celui que marque le compteur. Normalement, c'est deux cents, deux cents cinquante francs environ.

While killing time in the departure lounge of the airport, you could not help listening to someone who seems to be raving about something. Identify the key words and guess where they have been. The answer is on page 78.

... et les gens sont vraiment très gentils et pas aussi réservés qu'on le dit. L'hôtel était sur la plage et ou le temps merveilleux, nous avons fait beaucoup d'excursions dans la campagne qui est très belle et visité un tas d'endroits intéressants. Et le dîner à l'hôtel, vraiment très bon – rien à redire et pas cher. C'est pourquoi nous avons décidé tout de suite: l'année prochaine nous reviendrons sûrement à ...

◘ Let's speak French

A five point warm-up. Answer these questions using the words in brackets.

1 Il a acheté l'appartement à Marbella? (Oui, lundi)
2 Vous voudriez partir en Italie? (Oui, mardi)
3 Il sait que vous venez? (Oui, ce soir)
4 Pourquoi réparez-vous toujours votre voiture? (parce que, vieille)
5 Il a pris le train d'abord? (non, le métro)

In your last exercise you are going to interpret again, this time telling your French friend in French what others have said in English (the bit in brackets): Each time say the whole sentence OUT LOUD.

6 Quelqu'un dit que vous êtes fou (*if you buy this house*)
7 Quelqu'un dit qu'il n'aime pas ça (*if you come late*)
8 Quelqu'un dit que la douche est en panne (*if you don't have hot water*)
9 Mon ami a dit (*that our holidays are over*)
10 Elle a dit aussi (*that we are going to France next Christmas*)
11 Ma femme voudrait dire (*that she has (a) flu*)
12 et qu'elle ne peut aller (*because she is often sick*)
13 Mes parents ne peuvent pas aller (*because they are old*)
14 Mon ami dit (*that you are very beautiful*)
15 Il dit aussi (*that he would like your number*)

Answers

1 Oui, il a acheté l'appartement lundi.
2 Oui, nous voudrions partir mardi.
3 Oui, il sait que nous venons ce soir.
4 Je la répare toujours parce qu'elle est très vieille.
5 Non, d'abord il a pris le métro.
6 ... si vous achetez cette maison.
7 ... si vous venez tard.
8 ... si vous n'avez pas d'eau chaude.
9 ... que nos vacances sont terminées.
10 ... que nous allons en France le Noël prochain.
11 ... qu'elle a une grippe.
12 ... parce qu'elle est souvent malade.
13 ... parce qu'ils sont vieux.
14 ... que vous êtes très belle.
15 ... qu'il voudrait votre numéro.

Test your progress

I have crammed a lot into this last test – all 30 **Instant** verbs! But don't panic – it looks worse than it is. Go for it – you'll do brilliantly!

Translate into French, in writing:

1 We write a lot of letters because we have a computer.
2 How are you? What is the matter? Can I help you?
3 We are coming with a lot of people from the office.
4 He said that we are going to eat with friends.
5 During the Christmas holidays there is always a lot of snow.
6 The second case is in the bus. Can you take the black bag?
7 That's crazy: I believe that somebody has eaten my steak!
8 Why did you not telephone? We waited until yesterday.
9 Quickly! Have you seen a taxi? My plane is waiting.
10 I know it. The airport is always open – day and night.
11 I have worked on a boat but the work was not well paid.
12 I would like to eat (dine) later. At half past eight. Is that all right?
13 Your mother is very nice and she makes wonderful cakes.
14 Have you taken a flat in London or on the coast?
15 We must work a lot of hours. Three boys and two girls at school – that's too much money.
16 I hope that the garage can repair it.
17 I know her. She always goes shopping with her dog.
18 Who said that nobody can (not) smoke here?
19 I would like to speak with the sales assistant please. He gave me *green* shoes!
20 They say that you bought another Citroën.
21 What would you like to drink? We have a superb red wine.
22 Sunday and Monday the boat leaves at a quarter to six.
23 I am sorry, but **Instant French** is finished.

Check your answers on page 77. Then enter a final excellent score on the Progress chart and write out your Certificate.

answers

How to score

From a total of 100%
- Subtract 1% for each wrong or missing word.
- Subtract 1% for the wrong form of the verb. Eg. 'je sommes'; 'nous suis'.
- Subtract 1% every time you mixed up the past, present and future.

There are no penalties for:
- wrong use of all those little words, like: **le, la** etc/ **un, une/ de, du** etc/ **son, sa** etc.
- wrong ending of adjectives like: **'une maison bon'**.
- wrong choice of words with similar meaning like: **à, en, dans, chez**.
- wrong verb form – as long as it *sounds* the same, like '**je peut**' instead of **je peux**
- wrong or different word order.
- wrong spelling, missing accents, missing apostrophes, missing hyphens – as long as you *say* the word correctly.

> **100% LESS YOUR PENALTIES WILL GIVE YOU YOUR WEEKLY SCORE**

Week 1: Test your progress

1 Bonjour/allô, nous sommes Helen et Paul.
2 Je suis de Marseille. Vous aussi?
3 J'étais à Cannes en juillet.
4 Mes parents ont une Rover.
5 Nous allons à Nice avec la Renault et cinq enfants.
6 Je n'ai pas un bon poste.
7 J'ai besoin d'une maison pour les vacances.
8 Que faites-vous? Vous travaillez avec ordinateurs?
9 Elle a deux postes et trois téléphones.

10 Excusez-moi, êtes-vous Madame Cardin?
11 Nous travaillons chez Renault. Le travail est bien payé.
12 Nous avons un ordinateur très cher.
13 Je suis en France, mais sans ma femme.
14 Nous étions sept mois à Paris. C'est beaucoup.
15 Je vais à Nice. C'est très beau en avril.

> Correct your answers.
> YOUR SCORE: _____ %   Then read them out loud twice.

Week 2: Test your progress

1 Nous voudrions prendre un café.
2 Il y a une banque par ici?
3 Nous allons manger quelque chose.
4 Vous avez l'addition pour le thé, s'il vous plaît?
5 Mes enfants n'ont pas assez d'argent.
6 À quelle heure sommes-nous au bureau?
7 Ils vont toujours au café à six heures et demie.
8 Une autre question, s'il vous plaît: où sont les toilettes, tout droit?
9 Vous allez à Oslo en janvier?
10 Elle va à Los Angeles avec son mari.
11 Le petit déjeuner est superbe. C'est combien?
12 Où êtes-vous demain à dix heures et demie?
13 Il n'y a pas de poste sans un ordinateur.
14 Je vais au bureau et ensuite en vacances.
15 Excusez-moi, nous avons seulement une carte de crédit.
16 D'accord, nous prenons la Renault pour deux jours.
17 Nous allons réparer la Citroën. Elle est en panne.
18 Je travaille douze heures. Nous avons besoin d'argent.
19 Quinze francs pour un thé froid? C'est trop!
20 Il y a trois cents cafés par ici, un à deux minutes d'ici.

> YOUR SCORE: ___ %

Week 3: Test your progress

1 Vous avez vu un vendeur?
2 A quelle heure devez-vous aller au bureau aujourd'hui?
3 Qui a vu Pierre hier à la télé?
4 Je crois que les magasins sont ouverts maintenant.
5 Il y a un grand magasin par ici ou au centre?
6 Excusez-moi, je dois aller à la poste. Vous aussi?
7 Où avez-vous acheté le journal anglais?
8 Le temps est mauvais aujourd'hui. Il fait froid.

9 Quoi? C'est tout? C'était très bon marché!
10 Un timbre pour l'Angleterre – c'est combien?
11 J'ai une carte de crédit: Il y a un distributeur?
12 Nous devons aller au pressing. C'est bien, pas de problème.
13 Vous avez un sac pour mes chaussures noires, s'il vous plaît?
14 Je crois que j'ai vu une pharmacie par ici.
15 Taille douze anglaise – c'est quoi en France?
16 Vous avez travaillé jusqu'à cinq heures ou plus tard?
17 Je suis désolé, nous avons mangé tout le jambon.
18 D'abord, je dois réparer le sac, et ensuite nous pouvons faire les courses.
19 Nous avons tout pris: de la bière, du vin et du fromage.
20 C'était un vendeur très sympathique.

YOUR SCORE: ___ %

Week 4: Test your progress

1 Bien sûr, le rendez-vous était mercredi au bureau.
2 La semaine prochaine? Non, ce n'est pas possible. Nous n'avons pas le temps.
3 Je voudrais un verre de champagne et ensuite une bouteille de vin blanc.
4 Pouvez-vous m'aider, s'il vous plaît. Quelqu'un a besoin du numéro du médecin.
5 Il a dit que l'église est très intéressant. Vous l'avez vu?
6 Nous voudrions manger avec vous lundi soir.
7 Où peut-on acheter des fruits et des légumes par ici?
8 Le distributeur est en haut, devant la sortie.
9 Nous prenons le poulet ou la salade au jambon. Le poisson est trop cher.
10 Je connais bien les vins de Bordeaux. Ils sont superbes.
11 Vendredi, nous allons chez le client. C'est une affaire très importante.
12 Je voudrais acheter quelque chose. Comment dit-on en français...?
13 Je n'aime pas la Mercedes. Je vais prendre la petite Peugeot.
14 Il dit qu'il a la grippe et qu'il n'a pas terminé le travail.
15 Tout le monde a téléphoné ce soir. C'est fou!
16 Qui a vu que le chien a mangé ma viande?
17 Il y a de la glace. Mais je n'aime pas la glace au chocolat.
18 Ça va? Vous êtes malade? Vous devez boire beaucoup d'eau.
19 Quand allons-nous à Lyon cette semaine et pourquoi?
20 Que faisons-nous dans cet hôtel? C'est horrible.

YOUR SCORE: ___ %

Week 5: Test your progress

1 A quelle heure est le prochain bus?
2 C'est combien un aller-retour?
3 Qu'est-ce que vous avez dit? Pouvez-vous parler plus lentement s'il vous plaît?
4 Je ne comprends pas pourquoi l'essence est moins chère en Amérique.
5 C'est interdit de fumer dans le métro.
6 Vite, voilà le train. Quai trois.
7 Cette boîte est pour les cartes postales? Une boîte jaune?
8 Allô, je viens de Calais. C'est le garage?
9 J'espère que ce n'est pas la dernière station-service.
10 Il fait très chaud cette semaine. Je voudrais un peu de pluie.
11 Elle n'a pas attendu le feu rouge. Et maintenant elle est à l'hôpital.
12 Nous n'avons pas vu beaucoup de soleil. Je ne suis pas content.
13 Elle parle et fume trop sur l'autoroute! Je vais prendre le train.
14 Nous sommes à la police parce que quelqu'un a pris notre téléphone portable.
15 Les billets sont bon marché si vous les achetez maintenant.
16 J'aime votre Ferrari. Elle était très chère?
17 Il y a une pharmacie derrière la rue principale, à côté de l'arrêt du bus.
18 Comment est la voiture? Elle est vieille mais le moteur est nouveau.
19 J'ai besoin de deux billets. Il y a des places non-fumeurs?
20 Excusez-moi, je ne connais pas la ville. Où est la gare?

YOUR SCORE: ___ %

Week 6: Test your progress

1 Nous écrivons beaucoup de lettres parce que nous avons un ordinateur.
2 Ça va? Qu'est-ce qu'il y a? Je peux vous aider?
3 Nous venons avec beaucoup de gens du bureau.
4 Il a dit que nous allons dîner chez des amis.
5 Pendant les vacances de Noël il y a toujours beaucoup de neige.
6 La deuxième valise est dans le bus. Pouvez-vous prendre le sac noir?
7 C'est fou. Je crois que quelqu'un a mangé mon steak!
8 Pourquoi vous n'avez pas téléphoné? Nous avons attendu jusqu'à hier.
9 Vite! Avez-vous vu un taxi? Mon avion attend.
10 Je le sais. L'aéroport est toujours ouvert – jour et nuit.

11 J'ai travaillé sur un bateau mais le travail n'était pas bien payé.
12 Je voudrais dîner plus tard. À huit heures et demie. Ça va?
13 Votre mère est très sympathique et elle fait un gâteau merveilleux.
14 Vous avez pris un appartement à Londres ou sur la côte?
15 Nous devons travailler beaucoup d'heures. Trois garçons et deux filles à l'école – c'est trop d'argent.
16 J'espère que le garage peut le réparer.
17 Je la connais. Elle fait toujours les courses avec son chien.
18 Qui a dit que personne ne peut fumer par ici?
19 Je voudrais parler avec le vendeur s'il vous plaît. Il m'a donné des chaussures vertes!
20 Ils disent que vous avez acheté une autre Citroën.
21 Qu'est-ce que vous voudriez boire? Nous avons un vin rouge superbe.
22 Dimanche et lundi le bateau part à six heures moins le quart.
23 Je suis désolé(e) mais **Instant French**, est terminé.

YOUR SCORE: ___ %

Week 6: Spot the Keys

1 It depends when you are going. Normally it takes 20 minutes. But if there is a lot of traffic and the bridge is clogged up, it takes three quarters of an hour. The price is registered on the meter. Normally it is about 200, 250 francs.
2 They had of course been in ... England!

Week 6: Say it Simply

1 Excusez-moi, j'ai un problème. Ici/ça, je ne sais pas ce que c'est. Peut-être du vin rouge, peut-être autre chose. Mais nous partons demain. C'est possible de le faire pour ce soir, s'il vous plaît?
2 Bonjour. Mon nom est ... Kate Walker. J'étais dans la chambre douze jusqu'à aujourd'hui. J'ai des choses dans la chambre mais je suis maintenant à l'aéroport. J'ai besoin de mes choses à Birmingham mais j'ai un avion à prendre. Pouvez-vous m'aider, s'il vous plaît? Puis-je vous donner mon addresse? C'est... Merci bien.

how to use the flash cards

The Flash Cards have been voted the best part of this course! Learning words and sentences can be tedious but with flash cards it's quick and good fun.

This is what you do:

When the **Day-by-day guide** tells you to use the cards cut them out. There are 18 **Flash words** and 10 **Flash sentences** for each week. Each card has a little number on it telling you to which week it belongs. So you won't cut out too many cards at a time or muddle them up later on.

First try to learn the words and sentences by looking at both sides. Then, when you have a rough idea start testing yourself – that's the fun bit. Look at the English, say the French and then check. Make a pile for the 'correct' and one for the 'wrong' and 'don't know'. When all cards are used up start again with the 'wrong' pile and try to whittle it down until you got all of them right. You can also play it 'backwards' by starting with the French face-up.

Keep the cards in a little box or put an elastic band around them. Take them with you on the bus, the train, to the hairdresser's or the dentist.

If you find the paper too flimsy photocopy the words and sentences onto card before cutting them up. You could also buy some plain card and stick them on or simply copy them out.

The 18 **Flash words** of each lesson are there to start you off. Convert the rest of the **New words** to **Flash cards**, too.

It's well worth it!

**Flash cards for Instant learning:
Don't lose them – use them!**

1 excusez-moi	**1** s'il vous plaît
1 malheureuse-ment	**1** aussi
1 mais	**1** dans
1 très	**1** beau, belle
1 pour	**1** le travail
1 que	**1** chez

please [1]	excuse me [1]
also [1]	unfortunately [1]
in [1]	but [1]
beautiful [1]	very [1]
the work [1]	for [1]
at, to (someone) [1]	what, *also*: that [1]

ne... pas 1	mieux 1
cher, chère 1	je 1
nous 1	vous 1
en panne 2	peut-être 2
réparer 2	où 2
ici 2	à gauche 2

better ¹	not ¹
I ¹	expensive ¹
you ¹	we ¹
perhaps ²	broken ²
where ²	(to) repair ²
on the left ²	here ²

2 assez	**2** combien?
2 seulement	**2** il y a
2 d'accord	**2** demain
2 autre	**2** à droite
2 ensuite	**2** quelque chose
2 trop	**2** un peu

how much, how many? [2]	enough [2]
there is, there are [2]	only [2]
tomorrow [2]	agreed, all right [2]
on the right [2]	other [2]
something [2]	next, then [2]
a little [2]	too much, too many [2]

3	3
aujourd'hui	timbres
3 tout(e)	**3** d'abord
3 après	**3** Mon Dieu!
3 jusqu'à	**3** ouvert(e)
3 je dois	**3** plus tard
3 un distributeur (de banque)	**3** le pain

3 stamps	**3** today
3 first	**3** all
3 My God!	**3** after, afterwards
3 open	**3** until
3 later	**3** I must
3 the bread	**3** a cash dispenser

une bouteille **3**	comme **3**
qui **3**	quoi **3**
le magasin **3**	hier **3**
boire **4**	quand **4**
bien sûr **4**	derrière **4**
en haut **4**	je connais **4**

3	3
like, as	a bottle

3	3
what	who

3	3
yesterday	the shop

4	4
when	(to) drink

4	4
behind	sure, of course

4	4
I know	above, upstairs

je peux/ puis-je?	la glace
la sortie	rien
malade	personne
pourquoi	quelqu'un
prochain(e)	devant
l'église	un poisson

the ice cream | 4

I can/
can I? | 4

nothing | 4

the exit | 4

nobody | 4

sick, ill | 4

someone | 4

why | 4

in front of | 4

next | 4

a fish | 4

the church | 4

la gare	comment?
là-bas	non-fumeur
l'arrêt	parce que
la boîte	celui-ci, celle-ci
plein(e)	notre
la voiture	vieux, vieille

how, what, pardon? ⁵	the station ⁵
non-smoking ⁵	over there ⁵
because ⁵	the stop ⁵
this one ⁵	the box ⁵
our ⁵	full ⁵
old ⁵	the car ⁵

la rue principale **5**	l'autoroute **5**
l'essence **5**	le dernier, la dernière **5**
j'espère **5**	attendre **5**
l'aéroport **6**	partir **6**
jamais **6**	ils disent **6**
les gens **6**	leur **6**

5 the motorway	**5** the main road
5 the last	**5** the petrol
5 (to) wait	**5** I hope
6 (to) leave	**6** the airport
6 they say	**6** never, ever
6 them	**6** the people

6 je sais	6 à Noël
6 un bateau	6 voici
6 merveilleux (-euse)	6 nous connaissons
6 venir	6 donner
6 je vois	6 souvent
6 pendant	6 l'appartement

6 at Christmas	**6** I know
6 here is	**6** a ship
6 we know	**6** wonderful
6 (to) give	**6** (to) come
6 often	**6** I see
6 the flat, apartment	**6** during

J'étais trois ans à New York. [1]

Je travaille pour la banque. [1]

J'ai un bon poste. [1]

Je n'ai pas une grande maison. [1]

Nous avons deux enfants. [1]

Nous sommes en vacances. [1]

Nous allons à Bordeaux. [1]

Avez-vous un téléphone? [1]

Elle a une amie. [1]

C'est très cher. [1]

I was in New York for three years. 1

I work for the bank. 1

I have a good job. 1

I don't have a big house. 1

We have two children. 1

We are on holiday. 1

We are going to Bordeaux. 1

Do you have a telephone? 1

She has a girlfriend. 1

This is very expensive. 1

Il y a un café par ici? **2**

à huit heures et demie **2**

à cinq heures et quart **2**

l'addition, s'il vous plaît **2**

Où sont les toilettes,
à gauche ou a droite? **2**

La chambre, c'est
combien? **2**

À quelle heure est le petit
déjeuner? **2**

D'accord, nous le prenons. **2**

quelque chose à manger **2**

Nous voudrions aller à... **2**

Is there a café around here? 2

at half past eight 2

at a quarter past five 2

the bill, please 2

Where are the toilets, 2
on the left or on the right?

How much is the room? 2

At what time is breakfast? 2

All right, we'll take it. 2

something to eat 2

We would like to go to... 2

Je suis désolé(e). 3

Je vais faire les courses. 3

Nous devons aller a... 3

jusqu'à quelle heure? 3

pas de problème 3

Qu'est-ce qu'il y a? 3

Qu'est-ce que c'est? 3

Les magasins sont ouverts. 3

Nous voudrions acheter 3
un journal.

le bus pour le centre ville 3

I am sorry. **3**

I am going shopping. **3**

We must go to... **3**

until what time? **3**

no problem **3**

What is there? **3**

What is that? **3**

The shops are open. **3**

We would like to buy a newspaper. **3**

the bus for the town centre **3**

Il est très sympathique. 4

Il dit que… 4

J'aime le vin rouge. 4

Vous pouvez m'aider, s'il vous plaît? 4

Comment dit-on … en français? 4

Quelqu'un m'a dit que… 4

Nous n'avons pas le temps. 4

la semaine prochaine 4

Je le connais. 4

Ce n'est pas possible. 4

He is very nice. 4

He says that... 4

I like red wine. 4

Can you help me, please? 4

How do you say ... in French? 4

Someone told me that... 4

We don't have time. 4

next week 4

I know him. 4

That's not possible. 4

Pouvez-vous parler plus ⁵
lentement?

deux aller-retours, ⁵
s'il vous plaît

deux places pour ⁵
non-fumeurs

Je ne comprends pas. ⁵

Où y a-t-il une station- ⁵
service?

Je crois que la voiture est ⁵
en panne.

Il n'est pas cher parce ⁵
qu'il est vieux.

Ce bus va jusqu'à la gare? ⁵

A quelle heure part le train? ⁵

Nous venons d'Angleterre. ⁵

Can you speak more slowly? 5

two return tickets, please 5

two non-smoking seats 5

I don't understand. 5

Where is there a petrol station? 5

I think the car has broken down. 5

It is not expensive because it is old. 5

This bus goes to the station? 5

At what time does the train leave? 5

We are coming from England. 5

Je ne peux pas attendre. 6

Pouvez-vous venir? 6

Il a leur donné le numéro. 6

Celui-ci est pour lui. 6

Pouvez-vous me donner…? 6

Je n'aime pas ça. 6

Qu'est-ce qu'il a dit? 6

une semaine à Noël avec moi 6

Nos vacances sont terminées. 6

Je ne l'ai pas vu. 6

I cannot wait. **6**

Can you come? **6**

He has given them the number. **6**

This one is for him. **6**

Can you give me...? **6**

I do not like that. **6**

What did he say? **6**

a week at Christmas with me **6**

Our holidays are finished. **6**

I did not see it/him/her. **6**

*This is to certify
that*

....

*has successfully completed
a six-week course of*

Instant French

with .... *results*

Date   *Instructor*